CU00763511

000000692007

Utterly Undiscovered

Paul Costello

Illustrations by Emma Hames

fineleaf

PUBLISHED BY FINELEAF, ROSS-ON-WYE

www. fineleaf. co. uk

Copyright © 2013 by Paul Costello
ISBN 978-1-907741-30-2

Design: Philip Gray
Typeface: Warnock Pro
Print: SS Media Ltd
Forest Stewardship Council certified paper

Published by Fineleaf Editions, 2013
Moss Cottage Studio, Ross-on-Wye HR9 5TB
www.fineleaf.co.uk   books@fineleaf.co.uk

British Library Cataloguing in Publication Data
A catalogue record for this book is available
from the British Library.

Except as otherwise permitted under the Copyright,
Designs and Patents Act, 1988, this publication may
only be reproduced, stored or transmitted in any
form or by any means, with the prior permission
of the publisher, or, in the case of reprographic
reproduction, in accordance with the terms of a
licence issued by The Copyright Licensing Agency.

The author

Since a teen rebel of the 60s, Paul has picked away at the curiosities of life, offering an entertaining, sometimes surreal take on the world about us. He is author of published magazine articles and short stories, writes and performs in musical theatre, and holds an MA in Writing. Always seeking fresh material, he travels extensively from his Herefordshire home. Utterly Undiscovered is Paul's first full length work.
www.paulcostello.me

The illustrator

A passionate artist and musician, Emma's current work includes Music Art on recycled materials and development with her own band of a debut folk-rock album. Formerly resident in Shropshire, Emma teaches in the south of France.
www.emjhames.wordpress.com

DUDLEY LIBRARIES	
000000692007	
Askews & Holts	
	£9.95
GL	

··· In the Beginning ···

Two distinctive books, red and green with "Visitors" in gold on the front covers, have re-surfaced with other memorabilia from a box under the bed. From New Zealand to Norwich, Buenos Aires to Bath, more than five thousand people left their mark. Shiny volumes, dripping with stories.

My Ledbury townhouse is getting a radical makeover. The magnolia that has taunted me for three years will be buried under Dulux Pacific Breeze and other far-flung colours, and I shall become minimalist Ikea. The bulky pine and mahogany furniture that once held pride of place in guest rooms at Cricklewood Cottage, perfectly matching its ancient oak and pitch pine beams, has had its day. Faces no longer come to mind, but memories shout out from the well-thumbed pages:

Thank you for all the lovely extra touches and helpfulness.
Kevin and Pam, Sydney, Australia.

Amazing garden and fantastic veggie breakfast.
Win and Jim, Lingfield, Surrey.

The most beautiful B&B we've ever seen.
Doris and Sven-Olaf, Monchengladbach, Germany.

What more could you wish for?
Gerry and Barbara, Burnley, Lancs.

A wondrous place.
~~Billy Fury~~. My mum.

Absolutely gorgeous. Us all over.
Frank and Pam, Busselton, Western Australia.

I like Australians. And my mum. Billy Fury wasn't bad either.

How on earth did we arouse such passion, simply by feeding five thousand and finding them a place at "the inn"?

It was twenty years ago we first set foot on Shropshire soil. But it might have been yesterday . . .

··· To the Edge of Civilisation ···

We'd scoured the country looking for somewhere to resettle. Not that we felt compelled to leave Brighton – quit two well-paid jobs, sell our Edwardian town house and abandon families and friends. It was simple economics. By crossing the Great Watford Divide – selling at a silly southern price, buying at a crazy northern one – we could fund our plan with the leftovers.

Debbie was reluctant to leave her family in Lewes, so we struck a deal. I could run a Bed and Breakfast – but it would have to be in the countryside, where Debbie could sell crafts and create a garden. Not exactly what I'd had in mind, but come to think of it – crafts, cream teas and plant sales, as *well* as B&B – kerching!

Prime tourist areas like York and Chester had seemed a good bet. We looked at up-and-running businesses, only to find seedy rooms, seeping damp and the hollow black eyes of owners who couldn't cope. This convinced us to start from scratch, smaller scale, and make it our home not just a business.

When geographically challenged estate agents in Chester sent us properties for the entire hundred and seventy miles of the Welsh Border, we headed west and stumbled into Shropshire and Herefordshire. They say with relationships, the perfect partner comes along when you're not looking. Just so with houses. Expecting nothing, we fell for an eighteenth century country cottage with a babbling trout brook and a blank canvas of grass. Before we knew it we were proud residents of Plox Green.

'Plox Green?' people back home said. 'That's a weird name.'

'Yes,' we replied, enthusiastically. 'And you'll never believe what it's like! We're really close to the edge of civilisation!'

Sefton House, as it was known, had tremendous potential. Leaded windows, exposed oak beams, a huge inglenook fireplace and stunning views up to the craggy Stiperstones Hills. Although previously a happy family home, for our purposes the cottage needed a complete makeover.

The local builders, from Wembley, began adapting the cottage before we moved. Richard and Martin skilfully re-jigged the bedroom space and created a proper bathroom. There were few blips but panic set in when Richard phoned us in Brighton.

'It looks like dry rot in one of the bedrooms.'

What he meant was the floorboards had the appearance of dry rot – yet it wasn't. New boards were needed, but it could have been much worse.

Still committed to Council jobs in Sussex and our house unsold, we applied finishing touches on weekend visits. Debbie papered with Colefax and Fowler and crafted the soft furnishings, while I toned Council-stunted muscles scraping tarry gunge from beams to expose wonderful, oaky grains, missing for years. Outside, a coat of Dulux gave the cottage a brilliant white smile.

All under Jack's watchful eye.

Jack and his family live next door. It's a quirky set-up. Their bungalow overlooks our garden with a window the size of Woolworths and a boundary wall only two foot high. So *they* have a fabulous view of our planting schemes and *we* have a giant screen through which to view their everyday life – like watching a soap on mute. We hardly notice the lack of privacy though – it's so wonderful to be here. Quick-growing shrubs will do the trick. And natural repellents – like gardener's bum.

Jack built the bungalow forty years ago for him and his wife, Violet, and her sister Gladys, names reminiscent of the Brighton Belle's cream and brown Pullman cars that roared through Hassocks station when I was young. The walls are black-painted timbers set in white-painted concrete, and the roof has cedar tiles, called shingles, which curl up like bacon when it rains. In these parts you build as you go, using whatever materials are to hand. The bungalow appears solid enough, but its construction is distinctly Heath-Robinson.

Jack's career had been with a local building company, so his "material to hand" had been the daily surplus on the back of his lorry. Tucked away in various parts of the garden are stashes of black or red bricks, orange quarry tiles, granite cobs and rolls of square fencing wire, all grown around with grass and nettles. As you pull aside the undergrowth it's like a rare archaeological find.

Along the brook, camouflaged in a glade of tall conifers, is the wood and plumbing department. Thick rafters and wooden beams, steeped in wet rot and worm, nestle alongside earthenware drainage pipes and grey plastic guttering, disappearing up under the protective canopy of trees.

Jack says to let him know if I want any advice. There's little he doesn't know, and what he doesn't he makes up. We get the feeling he teases us southerners, accustomed to Building Regulations and B & Q.

'Ee'm the proper stuff, mark my word,' he says, handing me a small, sticky bag; so I follow his advice to use the thick brown resin as electrical insulation on our house sign. And though I'm reluctant to discharge kitchen waste water through an ancient underground pipe directly into the trickling brook, Jack assures me:

'That's the way round here. Everyone up the valley does it, mark my word.'

I mark his word. The honest grin and shiny, apple-red cheeks convince me all is well.

The inside of the bungalow is Violet's territory. A short lady with a firm chin and life-worn complexion, you challenge her well-grounded regime at your peril. Prescribed mealtimes mustn't be missed, the Hoover screams at half past ten, and waxy high polish wafts from an open door.

Just as the big screen is perfect for monitoring our garden at the back, the window above Violet's kitchen sink is an ideal lookout over the car park.

'See you bought Whiskas,' she calls, as I unload the shopping.

'Yes, it's on offer.'

I struggle with this sort of conversation. It's like living life twice – once in real time, then running through it again in case you missed something. You could easily halve your waking day.

'Drove in then?'

'Yes – took the car.'

'Shroosbury was it?'

Jack had told us it was called Shroosbury round here. We've always said "Shrosebury" because the BBC do. But the locals must be right, so Shroosbury it is. I have a hunch this will crop up with everyone who stays. It's one of those words.

'Yes, Shroosbury,' I say, feeling life ebb away.

For many years, Gladys was the village butcher; not in the sinister sense like Sweeney Todd, but running a place selling meat. The shop frontage on the outskirts of Minsterley, long since in residential use, still evokes images of post-war country life. Of fulsome build and severe in manner, I picture Gladys hacking at carcasses from nearby farms and gutting rabbits or pheasants from a local shoot. Though now sedentary and overlapping the polished wooden arms of an easy chair, a chance glare leaves me as wary as customers might have been, hearing the thud of Gladys's cleaver or seeing a boning knife pointed suspiciously in their direction.

A sturdy trio in their latter years, our neighbours dedicate themselves to dispensing encyclopedic local knowledge to anyone who'll listen. In other words, gossip. Like many locals they rarely visit the wonderful market town of Shroosbury, only ten miles away, though Violet makes a monthly mission on the bus, a salvaged 1950's coach with crunching gearstick and billowing exhaust.

'We dunna like the traffic,' says Jack, with a Welsh twang. 'Very busy, mark my word.'

Occasionally, they pile into a camper van for a risky trip to Aberystwyth; risky because the van is as old as the bungalow, and because the road skirts unknown terrain. Much of Shropshire remains undiscovered, and the locals do all they can to keep it that way. Rumour has it that in the hills some folk have never strayed beyond the local postbox. To us foreign-holidaying townies that's a scary thought!

'Shropshire? Where on earth is Shropshire?' friends had asked when we announced our leaving. Even we had to grab an atlas to explain. Shropshire is so uncharted it's a wonder we found it at all. The rotting wooden signpost at the nearby country crossroads says Shroosbury in our direction and Utterly Undiscovered in the other three. Our cottage was just inside the boundary of unexplored territory. Any further would have meant staking a claim for new land.

⋯ A Hedgerow of Sloe Gin ⋯

Our other neighbours, Geoff and Colleen, live down the lane opposite. Geoff farms the fields around the cottage, his muscular frame befitting someone toiling with animals and heavy machinery twelve hours a day. Coleen is small and tidy, scholarly looking with short hair and wire-framed spectacles.

They have us round for evening drinks one Friday. We'd planned exploring the village pubs later, but their home-made produce is pretty moreish – elder wine and sloe gin and crab-apple cider and . . .

'Try this,' says Geoff. 'From last year's strawberry crop. Forty-proof.'

'Oh thanks. Lovely colour. Mmm!'

We mention going for a pint at the Rowan Tree. They say there isn't a Rowan Tree; it's the Crown and Sceptre with letters missing. They don't force us to stay, but well, it's all rather nice.

'Have some parsnip liqueur,' says Colleen. 'It's got quite a kick.'

Four hours and forty anecdotes later we're best friends. Colleen is a keen gardener, so her conversation with Debbie is laden with Latin plant names which get harder to say by the minute.

'Sher-a-to . . . Ce-ra-to . . . shtig . . . – no, I can't say it, you say it.'

'Easy. Ce-ra-to-shtig . . . shtig . . . stig-maGrifth . . . Griff-ith-ii.'

'Horrible plant, anyway.'

'Yeah, I wouldn't have one.'

They give us gossip about our previous owners, who still live locally, and we share with them a vague version of our own plans.

Colleen says we say "right" a lot, and wonders if it's a southern trait.

'Really?' we say.

She says we also say "really" a lot.

'Really? Right!' We all laugh.

By half past eleven we are staggering and starving. The pubs will be closed but not the Friday chip van. Debbie and I stumble the mile to the village, delighted to have made new friends, and join a queue at the steps of the adapted 1930's country bus. Like us, half the village is desperate for something to soak up the alcohol. Gibberish fills the air. Folk disappear through the saloon-style swing doors and re-emerge triumphantly from the vinegary mist like aliens from a spaceship.

"Fish and chips" is hard to say after a hedgerow of sloe gin. But since you get the same whatever you order, I make a general "i" sound. Never has newspaper-wrapped saturated fat tasted so delicious or worked such miracles.

The following morning the cottage is like the sloth house at a zoo. We crawl from sofa to kettle and back to sofa. Conversation is sparse. In Brighton, Friday night's excess would have kept us in bed all day, but here there are things to do.

At ten o'clock the door bell rings. Geoff stands there with a boyish smile, and a powerful chainsaw hanging from his tanned arms.

'You said you wanted those trees taken down, so I thought we could do it now – if that's okay?'

'Right. I'll be out in a minute,' I say, charmed by his soft Shropshire dialect.

Debbie and I piece together the evening's conversation. It seems we discussed how a stand of mature ash and sycamore on the far bank of the brook spoilt our view. Because that was Geoff's side, he'd offered to take them down to use as logs in their wood burner.

Not an inspiring hangover cure, but I have no choice. By nightfall we are delighted with the result. Eastern light floods into the cottage, the view to the hills is magnificent, and we've bonded further.

A week later we finally explore the Minsterley pubs, meeting Richard and Martin in the Bath Arms. As well as their favourite watering hole and darts club, it's also a trading base.

'I can do that for you,' we hear, as Richard plies his trade. He's an electrician but turns his hand to anything. To us this is risky since the locals are hard to understand and he might not realise what he's agreeing to. The cross between Welsh, Scottish and local accents means we're still trying to interpret one sentence long after the next has started. The words "munna, canna, woona" flow into each other, soft and soothing as a hooting owl but impossible to decipher. Even a short conversation is a struggle.

'Oom err?' asks a wiry young regular with a squeaky voice. Roy's forehead is too big for his face, and he has an unsettling stare, but he does know everything about Range Rovers. We're still trying to work out his question when Richard steps in to introduce Debbie.

As the skinny landlord from Preston dispenses pints, The Who and The Beatles belt out from the busy juke box. During the silence of record changes, we catch cannas and munnas, insisting you can't or mustn't do something, and ee'm and err'm prefacing gossip about him and her.

We're surprised a small village has three pubs right next to each other when they're closing throughout the country. Locals drift between The Bridge, The Bath and The Crown and Sceptre (or Rowan Tree), a circuit known as the BBC. We join the flow.

The atmosphere in The Bridge is like The Bath – thick smoke, local banter, lively music and the continuous rush of beer pumps. There we meet Evan Davies. Although he's local, and like most villagers including Colleen, works at the sprawling Eden Vale Dairy (or Creamery as it's known) on the outskirts of the village, Evan's dialect is Welsh. Stripy braces support baggy, brown woollen trousers worn shiny at the seat and drawn well above the waist, over a short-sleeved, off-white undervest, buttons undone at the front. On top is a grey cloth cap and below are matted, maroon house slippers. Evan looks a dapper sixty something. Chinese whispers have told him everything about us.

'You'm from London then.'

'Well, sort of – Brighton actually but yes, the south.'

'I hope you'm ready for winter.'

'Why what happens?'

'Snow! Ee'm bad 'ere.' And he cites unofficial snowfall data from the early fifties – meaning we'll surely be holed up from October to April.

'Really? Right.'

Then he lists our jobs.

'You'm a teacher then,' he tells me.

'Er no, who told you that? I've never taught in my life.'

'Aar, that's what they said anyway,' he says.

'You'm a flower grower then. You'm opening a shop,' he says to Debbie.

'Well I like gardening, but no – no shop.'

'Aar, that's what they said anyway.'

I don't ask who "they" is. I explain that we're starting a new life and turning our hands to anything we can, which might include Debbie selling crafts and us taking a lodger. We're happy for that version to circulate, but don't expect it to stay the same for long.

Last orders are called and the chippie beckons. Our initiation is over; the Rowan Tree will wait till next time. As folk drift away, their farewells hang on the draught from the door.

'Duh-darr.'

'Duh-darr.'

'Ta-tar!' I call back. 'Shanna be long m'sen.'

We have new friends, and a new language to master. I'm getting the hang of it already.

··· Slithery Seltzer ···

'Oyez, Oyez, Oyez!' shouts the Town Crier, as the Mayor steps up to perform the ceremony.

Jubilant crowds line the streets. Bright bunting flutters from windows and trees.

'It gives me great pleasure . . . on this auspicious occasion . . . to declare Cricklewood Cottage . . . fully open!'

Snapping from my daydream, I step off the paint-spotted ladder to admire my handsome sign on its hangman frame.

1st August 1988. Three months since we arrived, and we're open for business.

Geoff waves from his tall tractor cabin, three Shredded Wheat bales spiked high on the front. He shows little surprise. We've dropped hints about "the occasional guest", and he and Colleen welcome the idea.

I wait at the window for a rush of customers. Jack is first to arrive.

'You'm doing Bed and Breakfast,' he tells me.

'Yes, we've got a spare room if anyone needs it,' I say, playing down our plans.

'Good idea,' he says. 'Not much B&B round here.'

Jack's reaction is encouraging. Living so close we thought they might feel threatened. Letting two or three rooms shouldn't affect neighbours, but fear and prejudice are funny things and it only takes one grumpy person to spread unhealthy rumours. Jack will tell people the truth:

'They'm okay.'

Across the road from Jack and us is Tollgate House, the third property making up our mini-community. Once a toll-house for the main road through Hope Valley to Bishops Castle, it has long since been a private residence, with an identical house the other side of the hills marking the southern entry of the old toll road, hemming it in like neat bookends. Now empty and for sale, only the ghosts of Victorian toll collectors will notice the comings and goings at our cottage.

And we've avoided the prying eyes of Council officials. I've checked that a B&B our size doesn't need planning permission, food hygiene inspection or a fire certificate. Not that we'd have minded, but we've just left officialdom behind for a *better* life. And aside from the expense, a stainless steel kitchen and thick fire doors would spoil the ambience we've carefully created.

After an hour, nobody has stopped for B&B, and I start to worry. Richard calls in to wish us well.

'I'll sort it out!' he says with the cocky assurance of an East Enders actor. Stepping onto the road, he flags down cars and points at the B&B sign, getting a few strange looks but not much else. At least he lightens the moment.

'You can't expect people to stop just because you've put up a sign,' he says, more life-savvy than me.

He's right of course. But I've waited a long time for this and need a customer to tell me how wonderful everything is. For today though, I'll settle for a brand new cottage sign as a mark of how far we've already come.

I never remember thinking, 'When I grow up, all I ever want to do is run a Bed and Breakfast.' But staying in B&Bs every year in Devon or Cornwall when I was young must have left its mark. Aah! Dear old Mrs Hooper in Tintagel – she did lovely jam tarts.

Frankly I never knew *what* I wanted to do. I only chose Economics as a degree because I'd done it at A-level, and only did it at A-level because Brighton Tech had little choice of subjects. And I only went to Brighton Tech because they threw me out of Grammar School where I was doing A-level subjects I didn't want to do because you couldn't mix History and Geography.

My parents never used the 'C' word. My early job changes, often involuntary, and the long gaps in between when I'd hitch-hike for fun to wherever the next lift took me, were not a career as they knew it. They chose the 'D' word – Drifting. I think my dad, who'd had a solid career in banking, was proud I'd studied economics. I went through the post-graduation motions of applying for jobs in ICI and Marks and Spencer, and even went for a teacher's training course in York. But my heart wasn't in it, and they saw straight through me at interviews.

I rejected the "get a good job, do well" school of thought, not in an anarchic sense – though at seventeen I *was* teetering on the edge of mods and rockers battles on Brighton beach without knowing which I really was – but in the sense of not wanting to be placed like a puppet in a box. It was the sixties – and I wanted to be out there, on an adventure!

In my early twenties, Dad, Mick and I made a plan. We'd buy a country pub. I had a Degree in Economics, my brother a Diploma in Hotel Management, and dad the money. He would charm the customers front of house, Mick would do the catering and I'd be general manager. Simple!

The plan grew stronger each time we visited a country pub, and every gin-and-tonic-fuelled evening at home helped make it watertight. Yet it was never the same the next day – that's if anyone remembered – and gradually the idea faded away. With hindsight, the plan never stretched beyond whose round it was next, and it would have been a personal and financial disaster.

Dad stayed at the Bank of England, Mick became a foreign exchange dealer, and I sold Schweppes drinks to London's hard-nosed grocery managers. We were all free to continue enjoying life on the right side of the bar.

At some point in my Drift, I lost the will to persuade owners of Cash and Carrys in Barking's gangsterland that a cuddly toy gift was worth an order for twenty cases of Pepsi, and Drifted back to Sussex for a job in Personnel. Handling recruitment with seven others in an open-plan Council office gave me a sense of belonging, as did sweet Alison in Admin.

But the thought of working for myself, offering hospitality as a way of life, never completely left me. And John Seltzer revived it a decade later.

John Seltzer was slithery. Slithery as an eel. He only partly lived up to his curative name. Effervescent he wasn't; wet he certainly was. John's tongue didn't sync with his teeth, so dewdrop dribbles would gather at the corners of his mouth and a fine spray would occasionally shoot out. Before a meeting we'd arrange chairs to keep out of range, but if rogue consonants brought about a special delivery, we were good at swivelling our heads from side to side like Egyptian belly dancers to avoid the missile.

When he got anxious his whole face wetted, a damp glow building to a shiny coat across his high forehead and pink, chubby cheeks. We would ask awkward questions with the sole purpose of speeding this lubrication, and when the facial shine met the dewdrop dribbles, and dark patches mapped out his shirt, we knew we'd won.

Rumour had it he'd been selected as the best of a bad bunch at interview. We wondered what the others had been like. It wasn't our problem he'd been appointed Chief Personnel Officer above his ability. He was a kind and willing man, with a paunch suggesting he was well looked after at home if not by himself. But his inability to manage people, least of all us wily bunch, made him a good target.

It became my aim to get a management upgrade and, after a decent interval, a management restructuring that made my post redundant. A pretty good exit strategy, I thought. John played along, and in the general scale of slitheriness the plan went swimmingly. All the more so when my office supervisor and lover, Debbie, reprised the tactics, allowing both of us to leave with a handsome pay-off.

The timing was perfect. I'd observed the grinding-down effect of Council bureaucracy on longer-serving people around me, and didn't want to go down that road myself. Life in triplicate had become tiresome. I needed a greater challenge. The desire to work for myself had resurfaced as I approached forty, and Slithery Seltzer's presence gave me just the prod I needed.

May 1988 – Friday 13th. Unlucky for some, but good for me – a farewell speech in one pocket, a redundancy package in the other.

My thank yous were genuine, but I couldn't resist a touch of management lampooning, like:

'Warehousing for the elderly is a growing concern . . .'

Or should it have been:

'Where housing for the elderly is concerned . . .'?

The answer depended on how you chose to interpret a report about elderly people being forced to move out of Council care homes.

Slithery and the big bosses stayed tight-lipped, pretending not to understand my carefully crafted management-speak. Real pals sniggered. Discreetly though – they still had to work there.

I was to be my own boss at last. Colleagues called it my mid-life crisis, but it was themselves they were consoling, not me. I called it an itch that wouldn't go away.

⋯ Three Burly Builders ⋯

I try not to look crestfallen as I open the door. I'd waited two weeks for the bell to ring and, expecting to find a couple of sweet old pensioners, I'm faced with three Lancashire builders on a flooring contract at the Creamery. My smiley way is wasted; the cottage might as well have been a motel overlooking a power station.

Next morning as they wrestle their giant tipper truck out of the tight car park, I watch from the doorway like a dog whose owner is leaving home without them.

'No!' I cry, rushing past Debbie into the kitchen.

She looks confused. Like a cat with wind I dash back through the front door, waving an insignificant business card. My mission is for every customer to take away the cottage details, and with my first guests I nearly forgot.

'Wait! Wait!' I yell, running towards the truck, which jerks to a halt with a loud hiss.

'What's oop, mate?' he says.

'I forgot this,' I mutter from below.

High up through the cabin window, the tiny card is swallowed by a fat, calloused hand, and three burly builders stare at the "Wally" blazoned across my forehead.

I hadn't expected this trade. Nor was the cottage set up for it. The fine china antiques and lacy bedspreads were for people seeking a character cottage – beams, inglenook fireplace and a pretty garden.

I *had* hoped to attract people working locally, but at the posher end – sales reps and managers. The burly builders brought me back to earth; I realised the type of working person would inevitably reflect the location – Minsterley and its Creamery – and that it will be contractors who share our cottage and get us started. Since the Creamery helps find digs for these visitors, they put us on their accommodation list and word soon goes round. B&B from this source is steady. Sensing they don't particularly enjoy working away, I try to offer basic home comforts, and contractors prove to be good customers without whose trade we'd have had to dig deep into our cash reserve. And *that* is earmarked for an extension to the cottage.

The Creamery is a hotchpotch of storage tanks, stainless steel ducts and giant warehouses spread over the size of ten football pitches. Name boards like Ski and St Ivel conjure a yummy image, but the site is grey and forbidding – and it's the first thing you see on arriving from Shroosbury.

Chimneys of different heights rise like a bar chart, the tallest belching smoke from time to time. Fortunately they're downwind from Plox Green so we rarely pick up smells, but driving past can be cheesy, and worse is the smell from a giant extractor fan at the meat-packing factory next door. If the cooked tongue aroma gets through the car vent it's as if you'd strapped your face to an open tin of Ye Olde Oak Ham for twenty minutes – mediaeval torture.

Milk tankers go to and fro day and night. Small ones collect from local farmers and large tankers transport milk from other regions to meet the huge demand. Articulated lorries take away the end product, mostly yoghurt and fromage frais, for distribution to supermarkets nationwide, including most of the Marks and Spencer range.

I see why Minsterley has three pubs, a thriving grocer, Post Office and butcher. It's a working village – employment is high and wages good. Between them, the Creamery and meat-packers employ most of the population, the Creamery alone taking five hundred. If the factories didn't exist, the pubs and shops would suffer and the village would soon become run down.

Ron is a stainless steel worker specialising in dairy equipment. Like Richard and Martin, he's a born Londoner but prefers not to live there. He becomes a regular at the cottage, arriving Sundays from deepest Cornwall and going back Fridays. He loves the cottage and treats it like home, staying in a small downstairs room at the back with a view to the hills. One week he brings his wife and switches to the Tulip Room, one of the two doubles upstairs.

'Lovely rooms,' says Carol. 'What made you choose those names – Tulip and Bow?'

'The patterns on the wallpaper,' I say. 'More country-sounding than "Rooms One and Two".'

'And what about the cottage? Why Cricklewood?'

'We brought it with us,' I say, embarking on a familiar explanation.

Our house in Brighton was nameless when we bought it – simply 13 Hampstead Road. It had lots of original features – mosaic-tiled floors, etched glass over the wide front door, moulded ceilings, tiled cast-iron fireplaces and sash windows – but no name.

That is until I could no longer bear the sight of the flaking "13" on a rotting board strapped to one of the cream pillars at the entrance steps. Removing this, I was thrilled to find the name *Cricklewood House* printed on the wall underneath. Having delicately touched up the black lettering with a child's paintbrush, we traced its origin.

Our Edwardian terrace, built in the heyday of the railway era, was near the London to Brighton line and would have been lived in by railway managers or other middle class London migrants looking for a better life by the sea. Just as Victorian colonists chose familiar names in their new country to retain a homeland feel, so ex-Londoners brought their own nostalgia to Brighton.

Sefton is a Metropolitan Borough of Merseyside, and Sefton House doesn't evoke images of an idyllic Bed and Breakfast in rural Shropshire. We needed a more distinctive name with a country feel. Resisting clichés like Brook Cottage and Hill View, we decided to bring our own memories and call it Cricklewood Cottage.

Richard and Martin laugh. Coming from Wembley they know that nearby Cricklewood is a declining industrial district of North London. But none of the locals have heard of it (after all it is more than ten miles away) and most guests won't know it either. So they'll be offered the railway explanation. Or perhaps the fairy tale one beginning:

"Once upon a time, at the foot of a hill,
near a deep forest called Crickle Wood,
close to the land of Utterly Undiscovered,
lived a butcher called Gladys . . . "

I only see Ron first thing in the morning. He works long hours and is early to bed. He lets me choose what breakfast to cook him, always something warm and hearty. One day he tells me the latest whispers.

'Evan says you're turning this into a hotel. Fifty rooms and a swimming pool fed by the brook.'

'What, the guy with braces?'

'Yeah – tells stories all the time,' Ron says, chuckling.

It sounded like Evan had adopted him as a drinking partner at The Crown and Sceptre, the missing letters for which had now been found.

'Ha! You wouldn't want to swim in it though,' I say, picturing fried egg leftovers and greasy dishwater lapping round my Lilo as I sipped house champagne – that's if what Jack says is true about kitchen waste up the valley.

'Says he sees you coming.'

'Who does?'

'Evan.'

'What do you mean "sees me coming"?'

'Leading you on, an' that. Thinks you'll believe anything.'

'Does he?' I say, feebly, thinking it was me who fooled Evan, not the other way round.

'Just watch out, that's all,' says Ron. 'He might be cleverer than you think.'

Ron stays nearly a year and becomes part of the household. His weekly cheque is a godsend, and as a leaving gift he makes us two protective stainless steel covers for the outside spotlights. We miss him when his contract ends.

I told Richard about Ron's remarks when he came round with Martin to fit a new chimney liner to the inglenook fireplace. We'd seen signs of smoke damage and wall stains where the chimney ran through the Bow Room upstairs, and agreed that the remedy was to seal the chimney.

'Evan?' said Richard. 'He's all bullshit. He did the same to me when I first came here. He's all right. Don't take any notice.'

'So it's just harmless gossip?'

'Yeah! He does it on purpose. Didn't you realise that?'

'What do you mean?'

'He thinks he's being funny – saying outrageous things, waiting for you to laugh or answer back.'

'What, it's him starting off all the stories?'

'Can't you see? He's a good actor. If you don't laugh, he'll just make up more.'

'And he reckons I've been taking him seriously?'

'Don't worry about it,' says Richard, his usual way of moving the conversation along.

I feel a fool that for almost a year I've not been reading Evan right. My excuse was that I was treading cautiously, not wanting to offend local people. But they say salesmen are the most easily sold to – and much of my Drift to date had involved selling.

··· My Basil and the Pigs ···

Debbie had not been alone in pointing out my Basil Fawlty tendencies. Along with millions of other viewers we'd loved watching repeats of Fawlty Towers, and before we left Brighton I'd been the butt of many jokes about Manuel and the Major, with a few "silly walks" thrown in.

I'd had plenty of practice with the young English Language students we'd taken for three years in Brighton. I tried hard to break down the ruthless efficiency of humourless Hans from Germany, but couldn't crack his stout veneer. Though my impersonation of him was more subtle than Fawlty's goose-stepping round his hotel or his advice not to mention the war, Hans got worse as soon as he realised what I was doing. He stayed six weeks but it felt like more.

And I'd tolerated Mahmoud, the Egyptian, who at first seemed polite and co-operative, but was clearly a past master at saying black was white with an innocent, fat-baby-boy smile.

Then there was Stefano from Italy whose rich parents delivered him to our front room, from where the ermine-coated mother announced, 'He very good boy, no trouble, and he no smoke.' Stefano sat timidly in the corner and waited till the door closed behind them before taking out a fag. His teenage slothfulness around the house never quite matched up to his surname of Ferrari.

But Stefano was an angel compared with Durul the Turk. Durul was openly dishonest and disrespectful. The climax of his four-week stay was to leave cigarette burns and used matches across the bedroom carpet. Presumably this was his way of saying 'thank you' after we asked the language school to remove him when, although we'd asked him not to, he brought a young lady home overnight for the third time. Whether it was the same woman on each occasion we'll never know, but he wasn't even subtle about abusing our hospitality, since his bedroom backed onto ours leaving us in no doubt that he had company.

There were many young people who *did* turn out to be delightful guests. We had Eva and Herbert from West Germany and Marcus from Switzerland all staying more than once, and our reputation with the language schools was second to none. But in the same way that bad news hogs the headlines, it was the awkward students that stayed in mind.

Now, with the added pressure of relying on guests for a living, I was primed to pick off those I thought unsuitable. I never consciously set out to be like Fawlty, but as soon as we had a steady flow of customers, the comparisons grew. Whilst Sybil Fawlty had asserted that the important thing was to have all the rooms full and make sure guests paid their bills, Basil wanted to build up a higher class of clientele and cut out the riff-raff. Like him, I'd anticipated a better class of visitor, such as Sainsbury's customers or people like my Auntie Katie on The Wirral.

'Ooh, you've got everything just right, Paul,' they'd have said.

'Thanks, yeah, pretty good, isn't it?'

I might not have believed them but it would have been more inspiring than watching men shove down cooked breakfasts in silence and go to and from the Creamery like androids. I'd been disappointed when the three burly builders had set the scene for our first year, though I came to accept that contractors were my early pay cheque, and some like Ron more than made up for it. At least their predictable routine led to few problems.

It was with other guests that challenges arose. I could never have competed with Fawlty's obsession with airs and graces ('the people in room six have never sat on *chairs* before, and are the commonest, vulgarest, most nasty . . .'), but I ran him a close second when it came to Americans. Whilst Fawlty simply couldn't understand that a Waldorf salad didn't consist of half a grapefruit with a cherry in the centre, *I* had to deal with more fundamental issues of common courtesy.

Four fat Americans, accustomed to fawning service in swanky New York dineries, have dinner in a twee cottage run by a country oik – who can fawn for England if he chooses.

'Get me some water.'

'*Say please.*'

'We're finished here – these plates can go.'

'*That's why I've come to collect them, jerk.*'

No pleases, thank yous or appreciation of fine food. I am simply a conveyor belt. Back in the kitchen, self-medicated vin rouge between trips to the dining room and a good deal of ranting help me cope.

'Bloody Americans! Who the hell do they think they are, arrogant b ––'

'Ha ha! It's My Basil!' Debbie shrieks with delight, little knowing how the label would stick.

There's no let-up at breakfast.

'Can I get a poached egg in a cup?' says one of the Americans.

'You could try. I'll hold the cup and you keep throwing the eggs.'

'Your kipper fillets, are they in cans?' asks another.

'No, on plates, but I might have an old can in the waste bin you could use.'

The whole notion of kippers is British and slightly eccentric. An acquired taste – which like Marmite you either like or you don't – the traditional time for eating kippers is at breakfast when you might least expect their strong flavour to be palatable. In Fawlty Towers a whole episode was devoted to the subject, linked to a guest found dead in bed. My experience with the American was more short-lived.

'No, they're fresh,' I tell him. 'Strong tasting, smoky flavour. You either like them or you don't – one of those things.'

I fetch a sample from the freezer and dangle it before him. The fish brushes the tip of his nose.

'Terribly sorry, I did try holding it steady,' My Basil assures him.

He opts for a cupped egg instead.

And like cucumber or garlic, kippers do linger. I never actually met the man I felt most sorry for. His wife-to-be, complimenting us by choosing our cottage for a few days with her friends before the wedding, studies the breakfast menu on the morning of the big day. Everything must be just as she wants it.

'I'll have the kippers please.'

'You may now kiss the bride,' says My Basil to the absent bridegroom.

'How do you make your cauliflower cheese?' asks a woman one morning, pointing at the chicken-shaped blackboard.

'Er, with cauliflower – and cheese?'

"My Basil" is coming along nicely, especially at mealtimes. The fixed three-course dinner menu is displayed at breakfast so that guests can book for the evening. Contractors generally prefer a pub meal, but as we start attracting a wider range of customers, dinner at Cricklewood becomes more popular. It's good income but hard work.

'Oh, the traditional way,' I tell the woman. 'Country herbs and spices.'

I put "country" before everything now. It sounds great! Country cottage, country views, spicy country muesli, the country hedgerow jam I make and sell. Country rats, country septic tank . . .

'What? No bacon?' she says.

'Telling me how to cook in my own home?' says My Basil. *'Outrageous!'*

The customer is right of course. They always are. But I have to say no or it would be unfair on others who've already opted for my "country" cauliflower cheese.

'If there's no bacon, I won't bother,' she says.

'Please yourself.'

'Have a lovely day,' I say – with a country smile.

On another occasion, I do a starter of home-made tomato soup for five Yorkshire people:

> To a tin of good quality tomato soup, add skinned, country tomatoes, country garden herbs, a dash of Worcester sauce and seasoning. Garnish with a swirl of single cream and serve with country croutons.

The atmosphere is tense as I collect the half empty bowls.

'What were thut?' says one of the men.

'Tomato soup,' I say.

'It were disgoosting,' he says.

Thinking it's northern wit, I grin and join in.

'Ha ha! Good! Good!'

'Yes, it were disgoosting, were thut!' says another man.

'I hope the main course is better,' says one of the women.

'There's plenty of gravy if that's what you're after.'

I've pushed their culinary boundaries too far. The customer is always right. Tomorrow I'll switch to economy soup powder.

'It's called taste,' says My Basil. *'Something you obviously know very little about.'*

For a small B&B there's an exceptional breakfast choice. Classic bacon and eggs is always the favourite, but guests can pick freely from an extended menu.

For the man from South Africa it's not a question of selecting from the menu, but ordering all of it. To him it's like a self-service buffet – fill the plate and keep fetching more until you can't cope.

'I'll have the porridge, yoghurt fruit and honey and some fresh grapefruit,' he says.

I'm impressed by his healthy choice; until I come back and find him scouring the menu.

'Now I'll have the full cooked breakfast, with two fried eggs, and waffles.'

Breakfast Menu

Help yourself to juice, cereals etc., then choose whichever dish or dishes you like from the following:

- Traditional Cooked Breakfast - Sausage, bacon, mushroom, tomato and egg (cooked to your order)
- Vegetarian Cooked Breakfast - 'Meat-free' sausage and bacon, mushroom, tomato and egg (cooked to your order)
- Yoghurt, fruit and honey
- Porridge
- Eggs - Fried, scrambled, boiled or poached
- Fresh grapefruit
- Kipper fillets
- Baked beans on toast
- Waffles with maple syrup
- Croissants
- Crumpets with cheese
- Brown or white toast
- Tea or coffee (both available decaffeinated)

'Would you like the waffles on the same plate?' I ask. It's a serious question, but Mr Rugged Suntan's expression says, 'don't mess with me'.

His clipped demands and greedy eating dominate the dining room and kitchen. He shows no sign of slowing down; other guests have to wait.

'I'll have crumpets with cheese, and a croissant – oh, and a boiled egg with toast.'

'What, no kippers?'

His timid wife looks resigned. She eats well but doesn't make a show of it. I doubt that she got to the bedroom garibaldis in time.

After an hour he starts leaving food on his plate and the performance is over. 'Have a good journey!' I say, as they move on to rich pickings elsewhere. *'Mind you're not sick in the car, Moneysworth!'*

··· Jasper's Nappy ···

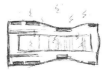

My carefully crafted advertisement for tourist brochures never made it to print. Debbie felt it might put people off.

> *Delightful eighteenth century cottage at foot of Stiperstones Hills. We welcome anyone with a pulse, and all pets, including ferrets, stick insects and goldfish. Open all year.*

But it had been meant in the Sybil spirit of getting bums in beds, and we genuinely welcomed any living creature. Well almost any – I'd worry if a wino turned up or someone smuggled in, say, a noisy parrot.

Friends and relatives from Sussex often came to stay. Emotionally, we'd disentangled from Brighton, finding it tired and grey after the violent storm of 1987, but we missed those we left behind. Asking them for money was never easy. Sometimes friends wanted to stay but not pay.

'Hello Paul – Roger and I thought we'd pop up to see you next Friday and Saturday. How are you fixed?'

'Yeah, be lovely to see you. There's a room free. Shall I hold it?'

'Yes please – if that's all right.'

'Er, I *will* have to ask you to cover the cost of the room, if that's okay?'

'Oh – right. Er – how much will that be?'

'Forty-pounds – altogether for the two nights.'

'Right. Er, yes. I suppose that'll be all right.'

I point out that customers are our livelihood and that two letting rooms is all we have. In reverse, the scenario would be:

'Hello Roger – Debbie and I are coming to Brighton next week. Any chance of meeting Wednesday or Thursday?'

'That'd be good! But we're busy those evenings and working during the day.'

'Any chance you could take time off?'

'We've used up our leave.'

'How about unpaid leave?'

'Very funny! Do you think we're made of money?'

They understand we have to make a living but don't quite know what that means. Most are employed, like we'd been, and don't appreciate our new way of "making a living". On a regular salary you know how much you're getting and spend it with confidence. Working for yourself you have to make the money first.

Debbie thinks we shouldn't charge them. She sees it as raising barriers to good friends. We agree to disagree. I point out they could stay free in winter when trade is poor, which of course none of them want to. And in the summer I offer a tent at the bottom of the garden if they don't want to pay.

'Love to see you!' I say to Chris, a friend planning a visit from London. 'You don't mind using a tent for a few days, do you? It's very spacious.'

'Ha ha! If you say so,' he says, used to my sense of humour.

On arrival I lead him to his living quarters, and he disappears inside with a questioning look.

Others unwittingly arrange "camping weekends", and the reaction is always: 'I thought you were joking.' I stress their good fortune – that they'll have something to tell their grandchildren.

Until we build the extension, guests share our living room, where I offer tea and garibaldis and riveting small talk. Conversation in a room full of newcomers can be fun. Perhaps one person dominates the conversation while others sit quietly. Or someone hard of hearing might make everyone else speak louder. A joke teller can become a pain – though never as bad as a colleague at Schweppes whose idea of spontaneity was to flick through a pocket notebook for the next joke.

'Now let me see. Ah yes, here's a good one. A man walks into a bar ...'

It can also be uncomfortable. A pair of young Born Again Christians, eager to espouse their cause, kept responding to other guests with, 'God has a reason for everything.' Another couple waited patiently for a lull in proceedings before asking, 'In that case, can you please ask Him why our twins have both got cerebral palsy?'

I slunk off to the kitchen.

One weekend towards the end of our first summer we have an interesting mix of new guests – an elderly couple on a short break, a young man on a sponsored cycle run from Edinburgh to Exeter, and a woman with a small baby.

I join them for tea and garibaldis. The focus turns to the baby and its mother, who is intent on sharing her views on birthing and motherhood. There's nothing she doesn't know on the subject, and when we find she's a family social worker none of us chooses to challenge her.

Having subdued the room, Earth Mother sweeps her wriggling, squiggling baby from its carry chair onto a plastic sheet in the middle of the floor, a perfect location for her captive audience.

Conversation dwindles and the show begins. We fiddle with teacups and shuffle in chairs, eyes dragged centre stage. The offending garment is whipped off, its gleaming contents waved in triumph as Jasper writhes with glee in the remnants, destined like his mother to become a great actor. Earth Mother warbles reassuring words that only *they* understand.

'Oo's a gorgeous little treasure? Oo's a smelly-welly, sweetie-weetie?'

'Obviously not us. We're just here to look and learn.'

'What we gonna do with you, eh? What we gonna do with you?'

'I've got a few ideas.'

She mops around, spreading the residue evenly before applying sweet powder and a fresh catch-all conjured from a Mothercare bag as expertly as the plastic sheet. Realizing we're hooked, she leaves the baby mid-carpet for all to enjoy.

The only other Jasper I've known was the family dog when I was nine. He kept chasing the farmer's sheep, so had to be taken away.

Emerging from our hypnosis, we stand and applaud Earth Mother and Jasper on a remarkable performance. I don't mention the dog.

Note to self: possible earner – charge for baby demos.

··· In Out, In Out ···

Money in, money out. In out, in out – that's what it's all about. Mr Micawber got it right – when money in is greater than money out, you're in pocket.

Once we add a third double bedroom there'll be more money in. But for now there's not enough, and we have to use our wits to make ends meet.

Debbie sets up her craft business, selling through local shops and craft fairs. Her dried flowers, stencilled mirrors and jars of pot-pourri, displayed near the breakfast table, are popular with guests too. And like the B&B, Cricklewood Crafts is eligible for Mrs Thatcher's Enterprise Allowance. She offers generous payments to unemployed people setting up new businesses – and we both qualify. Our heartfelt thanks go to Mrs T and of course Slithery Seltzer for helping fund our new lifestyle.

A year on, and money in to Cricklewood Crafts is less than money out. Competition is tough, profits small, and Mrs T's forty quid a week is only paid for a year. So Debbie stops trading and settles for a steady income from babysitting and cleaning.

I keep fit by working as a builder's labourer to Richard and Martin who are doing up a house near Oswestry. And I also find a great market research job.

'You'll have to drive around Shropshire inspecting advertising boards and telephone kiosks,' says the director of a Luton company on the phone. 'We'll supply a camera and pay you time and petrol. Are you interested?'

Being paid to explore my new county. 'Hm, let me think about that – yes.'

Later they add mystery shopping, where I have to pretend I want some make-up in Boots or a loan at Barclays, but really I'm scoring the staff on customer service. Ooh, the power!

The main money out is supplies, especially food. Conditioned by my years with Schweppes, and by Debbie's parents who ran a pub, I expect to get big savings buying in bulk from Cash and Carrys – assuming I can find one.

Shroosbury is closer to the civilised world than Plox Green (just), and Richard thinks there's a Cash and Carry to the north. After three circuits of the industrial estate I spot MOJO between the ATS tyre centre and a double glazing depot. Outside it's like a World War 2 aircraft hangar, inside as spooky as its name.

Stacked roof high are giant tins of vegetables, huge boxes of Kellogg's Cornflakes, and multi-packs of toilet rolls, not fours or nines but twenty-fours and thirty-sixes. Through a set of rubber doors in the cool room are whole meat carcasses on hooks and enough slabs of cheese for a life supply of Welsh rarebit.

It's nearly twenty years since I've been in a Cash and Carry. Now a customer not a rep, I feel more important. But I'd forgotten how vast and unfriendly they are. A background tang of damp and bacon; no windows; only bare bulbs somewhere above the boxes to guide a few dispirited customers through the gloom; the only sign of life a stop-start rumble of distant trolleys, their wooden slats and cold, iron push-bars polished through decades of use.

I trundle past bucket-size cartons of cheap soup powder and tins of economy baked beans big enough for a cowboy army. The prices are good but do I need it all and where will I keep it? And does it *really* look appealing?

Near the checkout I spot an Asian man, who appears to be the owner, dealing with an angry customer. It reminds me of my many Asian customers in the London grocery trade, though there's little sign of the same trend in Shropshire. A flimsy tee-shirt hangs shapeless on his squat physique, the dark top and shabby shell suit trousers camouflaging him in the dim interior. With a wobble of fleshy cheeks he sees off the customer. I scuttle away in case he turns on me for still having an empty trolley.

The chill atmosphere gets to me. This is not my world. I want to get away, but can't leave empty-handed – I'm a dynamic, new businessman, and want people to notice. Confident at the very least of getting through plenty of toilet rolls, I reach up a tall stack and tug at a shrink-wrapped pack of three dozen until the white tissue tumbles onto the trolley, adding two more to appear businesslike.

The spotty checkout assistant Dan, stares in turn at me and my hundred and eight toilet rolls as if demanding an explanation. Perhaps the owner has trained him to do that. Or maybe it's the look of someone who whiled away his CSE exams dreaming of a career in Cash and Carrys.

Worried the Asian man may step from a dark corner and ask awkward questions, I peel the notes off a roll in my shirt pocket and swagger back into a brighter world.

I still have to smuggle the bulky packages into the cottage without Violet seeing, which takes two furtive dashes down the back path overseen by Debbie, who has the same quizzical look as Dan.

'Is there something you're not telling me, Paul?' she says.

'Big savings, luv. They'll last three years.'

I split the packs and find them suitable homes – in the sideboard, under the bed, and along the entire top shelf of the airing cupboard. Tearing off a sheet to check its quality, I adjust my estimate from three years to three months.

'Don't know why you didn't get Izal and be done with it,' says Debbie. 'You could have used it as sandpaper too. That would have been better value.'

Later I pick up a scribbled note from the front doormat:

You'm all right for toilet rolls then

My brief love affair with Cash and Carrys over, I move to plan B – Kwik Save in the centre of Shroosbury. Like MOJO, this cheap supermarket has the motto: "Stack 'em high and sell 'em cheap", except that in Kwik Save you can buy normal amounts. And it has windows.

To reduce "money out" I use the nearest free parking, half a mile away up a steep road, through The Quarry – Shroosbury's town park – and over the River Severn via a squeaky footbridge with rusting bolts. The store doesn't have plastic bags; empty boxes for customers to self-pack are in a large bin by the checkout. So every week I take a pleasant stroll across the park with a cardboard box.

After we get a second cat, I can easily buy enough to fill two boxes, peering round the carefully balanced duo to make sure I'm heading in the right direction. People turn to follow my progress across the park as if I'm a straggler in some sort of triathlon.

As spring turns to summer, business picks up and I need three boxes. No longer able to see round the tower, I follow the tarmac path below as best I can. Word has spread, and small groups gather in anticipation every Thursday, their smiles and cheers spurring me on.

In time, it becomes a continuous throng, two or three deep, lining the road much as they do The Mall when royalty is due to pass. From the park gates I can hear the hum of the waiting crowd – women with children, joggers, dog walkers and shop workers using lunch breaks to witness the shopping phenomenon. Council gardeners lean on their hoes, and the ice cream man has a perfect view from the raised window of his van.

As I stagger past, applause ripples down the rows like a Mexican wave. If I falter with a particularly heavy load, someone from the crowd steps alongside to steer me towards the squeaky bridge. A small girl darts from the front to retrieve a can of Felix that topples from the overfilled top box, and has fun looping it back in. What a story to tell her grandma!

I save a fortune at Kwik Save. But my notoriety excites me more. Realising I could harness this to promote the B&B, I consider leaflet racks and logos on each box, twelve sides in all, a perfect place to create brand awareness as I lurch between thick rows of spectators each side of the road.

Instead I get so knackered I start going to Tesco – parking outside like everyone else.

Supermarkets offer good value, but not necessarily for fresh produce. I make a wonderful discovery three miles from the B&B. An independent grocer selling fresh fish, meat and home-baked bread – a family business of charm and distinction. Hignett and Sons of Pontesbury.

Chunky butcher's sausages on endless strings replace anaemic chipolatas with nought percent pork. And freshly sliced, water-free bacon means no more skinny rashers that drop through my grill into the fatty broth below.

'If I take twenty pounds of middle-cut and twenty pounds of pork sausages, what price can you do?' I ask Nick, mentioning the B&B.

'I can give you ten per cent for that,' he says.

Oh – I know how to get a deal! Bulk buying is quite the thing.

At home I split the forty pounds of meat into breakfast portions, sausages in pairs and a top and tail of bacon. Wrapping them and re-arranging the freezer takes an hour and a half and ten metres of cling film.

I repeat the order three times during the summer, and by autumn I'm buying all my meat, fish, fruit and veg, eggs and bread from Hignett's.

'Could I still have ten percent if I take just three pounds of each?' I say, expecting quieter trade.

'No problem!' says Nick. 'You should have asked before. We'll give you ten percent on everything you buy. That's what we do for other B&Bs.'

'Grr! Now you tell me!'

Like a child practising handwriting I enter every transaction neatly in the bright orange ledger my accountant told me to buy:

Money out

Personal	*Mars Bar 20p*
Provisions	*Honey £1*
Stationery	*Bright orange ledger my accountant told me to buy £7*

Money in

Home-made country jam   £1
Customer tip £1. 50

On one occasion I lump two Mars and a Twix together as a single entry under Personal Spending, and feel elated at taking such a bold step. As well as income and spending records, I keep statistics for advertising response using a simple, five-bar-gate system. This helps gauge value for money from paid advertisements, and what comes free from the B&B sign or word of mouth.

Debbie thinks I'm obsessed with money and accounting. When we had two good salaries we hadn't worried much about money out; there was usually plenty to go round.

'A penny is the benchmark,' I now say when she does the shopping. 'You shouldn't have to pay more than that per teabag.'

'Are you being serious?' she says.

'It's good housekeeping. What's good enough for Mrs Thatcher . . .'

And she's not impressed when I suggest using my barber, Gary, to trim her hair on Thursdays at the Crown and Sceptre. At a pound a go he's excellent value, and I don't get Debbie's point about pampering and ambience. Personally, I think waiting on a wooden bench in the back room of a pub alongside slurry-spattered farm hands and yoghurt-smudged Creamery workers, with Gary's belly nudging my arm as he moves around the chair, is what rural togetherness is all about.

A friend over from Australia takes financial control a step further than me, using a calculator to deduct spending as it occurs:

Bananas minus 20p

Two cups of tea minus 30p

Sitting in a Shroosbury tea room, Debbie and I watch him tap the keys and transfer figures to a pocket notebook.

'What you up to, Jim?' I ask.

'Budget, mate. Gotta watch the money. Especially after the twenty quid you charged me to stay. Don't you keep records?'

'Nah, mate. I'm cool about money. But you go ahead.'

Debbie gives me one of those stares. But Jim has taken the pressure off, making me look more laid back than the Maharishi Mahesh Yogi.

Debbie and I are different, that's all. While she's all chrysanthemums, crafts and Colefax and Fowler, I'm trying to turn pennies into pounds. As for keeping records – well, you can take the boy out of the bureaucracy, but . . .

··· Wake's Sludge ···

'Hello, you don't know me. I'm Lewis Wake.'

In stark contrast to the Evan Davies school of fashion, the man on my doorstep looks dapper in his creaseless, pale grey suit and black polo neck.

'Hello, how can I help?'

'I thought I'd let you know it's me who has the contract to remove Creamery waste. If it affects you, do tell me.'

'Waste?' I say, not liking the sound of this.

'Yes – it's part of the production process. Used as plant feed.'

'Exactly what do you do?' I ask, "plant feed" sounding a bit healthier.

'We take away the yoghurt refuse and spread it on the fields. Perhaps you've seen my tankers going past – the large, green ones?'

'Ah! So it's your *fat tractors I get stuck behind?'*

'Yes, I did wonder what was in them,' I say.

'I notice you do Bed and Breakfast,' he says. 'I wouldn't want to inconvenience your guests. I'll give you my number. If you have people staying let me know and I'll make sure I don't spread on the fields just here.'

Wake, as I find he is known everywhere – and he *is* known everywhere – is a total charmer. In his line of work he has to be. Third last in popularity after traffic wardens and tax inspectors (make that fourth – I forgot estate agents), he regales me with the nutritional value of his sludge. But I don't believe a word of it. I heard elsewhere that he pays farmers to lay it on their land; so the farmers gain, *he* gains, and anyone who prefers the smell of cooked cabbage to the scent of honeysuckle, lemon balm or sweet peas – gains.

Wake's visit proves invaluable. The spreading is done in rotation, so the fields by the cottage are only affected from time to time. But if I do see a tanker in the field and I'm expecting guests, a quick call and, true to his word, the offending vehicle disappears instantly, as if I had cast a spell from the kitchen window.

If only it was the same for chicken shit. Above a grass bank in the distance we can just see two huge chicken batteries. Like yoghurt sludge, the foul stuff is carted away and laid on fields as fertiliser, and of all animal refuse chicken is by far the most acrid. If it doesn't get washed in by rain, the throat-clenching stink stays in the air for weeks. And once they've absorbed a shedload of shit, my clean sheets and towels have to be re-laundered.

'Thanks for that, Mr Chicken Shit. Try Wake's book of country etiquette!'
Luckily the clearance is only two or three times a year. And I could always recycle "shitty" sheets onto the beds of guests who annoy me, I suppose.

Note to self: get used to country life.

A new decade, a new spring, and still nobody has mentioned smells or anything else peculiar to the countryside. But when it does come, the first complaint is a beauty.

'Your birds are noisy,' says a woman at breakfast.

'You mean the jackdaws?' I say. They'd started building a nest in the chimney and their raucous calls had echoed down the inglenook each morning, three times magnified, as if they were behind you.

'I removed the nest last week before they settled, in case we still light the fire,' I say. 'The chimney's wired now, but they still perch on it. Sorry about that.'

'No,' says the man. 'It was the *other* birds singing – when it gets light.'

'Sorry to hear that,' I say, realising they're serious. 'Well – that's the countryside for you.'

'It's called the morning chorus, sir.'

'Seemed a bit bloody loud,' he says. 'Are they always like that?'

'Oops, I think the toast is burning,' I say, leaving the other guests to explain.

Later I check their name in the Visitors Book. Mr and Mrs Robins. That figures. I'll send them a robin redbreast card at Christmas. One that tweets when you open it. Or perhaps I'll put chicken-shit sheets on their bed tonight – they're clearing the sheds this week.

I've kept a Visitors Book ever since we took the foreign students in Brighton. It's fascinating seeing where people come from and reassuring to know how many guests we've had.

The Tourist authorities say we should record all guests over sixteen by name, nationality and passport. When I ask why, they mumble about security and hotel legislation – loosely translated: 'tracking down illegal immigrants or criminals on the run'. I play down such bureaucracy – too Big Brother for our friendly image. We're not the same as a hundred-bedroom hotel, although Evan probably has us at that by now. If a petty official wants to inspect records, my version will do – name and address.

I don't encourage guests to offer comments in the Book because too often they're bland and meaningless:

> **_Comfortable and friendly_** (ordinary)
> **_Will definitely be back_** (a lie)
> **_Heaven-on-earth_** (ridiculous – American, of course)

We saw a lot of this in other guest houses. People say things for their own comfort, not ours. It's like leaving tips in a restaurant – conscience money. I could write a whole book on the subject.

But offer them they will, and to be fair some comments are heartfelt:

> **_Just as lovely_** My mum.
> **_Absolutely bloody marvellous_** Australian (Vintage).

I still like Australians. My mum's up there too.

The Visitors Book is also a source for sending Christmas cards. Direct marketing – like Indian restaurants but more of a surprise; in Indians they spoil it by asking for your address in November and telling you why. So shallow.

Except for the three burly builders who wouldn't understand, I send cards to everyone on our first two Christmases, but stop when I see little business gain.

'Anyway, don't you think it was a bit insincere?' says Debbie.

'Maybe – but worth a try. Don't you think it's a bit insincere sending cards to people you met once on holiday ten years ago and wouldn't be able to pick out in a line-up?'

'Well, they send _me_ one.'

'And handing office colleagues thirty identical robin redbreast cards with thirty identical messages?'

'Humbug!'

'And getting thirty identical ones back?'

Anyway, that subject too would take another whole book.

Visitor Book graffiti can also be a problem. Take Jim – at some point when he didn't have his head in a calculator he used our Book to hark back to school days:

> **_Doing well then, Costello, after "consistently refusing_**
> **_to be roused, led or driven"?_** – **Jim, Australia.**

He had extracted this from the final school report I got before being sent home from Brighton, Hove and Sussex Grammar School. It was the calmness of the headmaster's execution that made me feel helpless:

'Costello, I don't want you here anymore. Goodbye,' were Mr Brogden's last words as he turned away. Aah, Harry, if you could see me now.

I question how interesting other guests will find this sort of thing. Why on earth would they want to know I was caught smoking Woodbines at The Dyke Road Cafe when I should have been in History? Or how the uniform I wore on Fridays for compulsory Cadet Corps was thick enough to soften the pain when I was caned for reading the New Musical Express in Mr Smithies' English class?

That would need a book all of its own.

A more common observation is road noise. Heavy vehicles serving the Creamery tend to go the opposite way, and being on the edge of civilisation there's not much through traffic past the cottage, especially at night. Farmers start early and finish late; my morning call is not from a five quid Boots alarm but Geoff's tractor pulling away at six thirty-three on his way to milking the cows at six fifty-one. Throughout the summer he returns late after sowing or harvesting; and for as long as there's light, Wake's sludge will be on the road somewhere. But generally it's quiet.

Having previously lived by road and railway, Debbie and I slip easily into soundproofed sleep. But light sleepers, used to double glazing in a Cowdenbeath cul-de-sac, might resent the rumble of a sludge tanker grinding past or the screech of a boy racer taking the bend on two wheels at one in the morning.

Some guests hate it, some feel at home. It's one of those things. Like kippers.

⋯   A Dog Called Bite   ⋯

Our Pets Welcome policy means we often get dogs. Some guests who are used to B&Bs not taking pets, leave their canine cuties in the car. This suits us better, but we find that whilst dogs can be quiet when their owners are around, once separated they pine.

Dogs barking in a car park attract more than just their owners, who are least likely to hear since to them barking is as normal as shrieking is to mothers at a playgroup or the bass vibe to club goers – they only notice if it stops. A dog that pines will also be calling to Jack, Violet, Gladys, John and Meg our new neighbours at Tollgate House, guests, passers-by and us.

The crunch of feet on gravel is like a spark to touchpaper. So when our cats, Oliver and Thomas, use the car park for night hunting, or a lost hedgehog tiptoes past, or two pigeons have a punch-up on the bonnet at five in the morning, the dog is the appreciative audience. If he's also clever enough to trigger the car alarm, it can sound remarkably like the climax of Tchaikovsky's 1812 Overture.

Six a.m. Sunday morning, early spring.

'Damn!' says Debbie from somewhere under the pillow. 'My eye drops are in the car.'

'I'll get them before I do breakfast,' I say, knowing she'll want a lie-in after late-night babysitting. 'You don't need them now, do you?'

'My eyes are really sore. Do you mind?'

We've used Ron's old room since he left in December after being with us for most of 1989. A double bed just fits in, leaving a square foot to undress in.

We'd been forced out of our temporary camp in the store shed when temperatures plummeted to minus ten Celsius. Not that Evan's forecast had been accurate. In our first winter there was no snow and little frost. The snow shovel was still a virgin and I even had to trim the lawn a few times.

It had been an adventure sleeping in one of the rear add-ons with their wooden walls and corrugated iron or asbestos roofs. Our chosen lean-to, which had previously been used as a utility room, became the sleeping quarters and clutter dump. Attempts to make it homely, shoving carpet offcuts in the spaces and pictures between the cobwebs, were partially successful, and at least there was an old toilet.

Fabulous flagstones peeped through the ugly concrete skim where it had chipped away. The uneven floor sloped away from the main house at an angle similar to the lower reaches of the Stiperstones. Our folding camp beds only fitted lengthways along the slope, so if you turned downhill you rolled onto the floor. Too quick a turn and you'd have enough momentum to roll into Minsterley Brook had the wall not been strong enough between the woodworm holes to halt your progress. Turning uphill was like, well, trying to roll up the lower reaches of the Stiperstones.

'Where do *you* sleep?' guests asked, with curiosity and concern.

'We've got our own place out the back,' I'd say, leading them to believe for a while that we had a living area to ourselves – which in a way we did. Only when they walked past the back of the cottage to check out the giant screen they'd heard about did they twig on, and then they'd feel too awkward to say anything.

Our store-shed retreat was next to Ron's room. It seemed likely he'd have looked in sometime when we weren't there and politely said nothing, relieved to be offered better accommodation than ours. We spent many a night listening to his Snoring Symphony No. 1 (The Cornish) as we dropped off – and occasionally dropped off again.

In the November before he left there'd been a persistent cold snap. Though we'd got through one winter without mishap this was shaping up to be an Evan one. Frosts had started in late September and were by now unforgiving, radiating off the iron roof and firing a million skinny strands through the worm holes. The novelty of camping out had worn off.

As the frosts hardened, we got used to diving into bed quickly, fully clothed, and escaping just as fast in the morning. On the coldest nights our hair would freeze.

'Did anyone ever say you look like Ken Dodd?' a guest asks at breakfast.

'No, but one or two have said Debbie looks like Mrs Thatcher on a bad hair day,' I say, wiping the table where ice particles have dropped off my beard.

One morning in mid-December I woke up with frozen snot. Having a cold, it looked like I was growing stalactites. The duvet no longer had enough bend to tuck round me, and my lips were stuck together, except for a pursed bit in the middle which I could breathe through with fish-like gulps.

Debbie lay alongside with a hand to her forehead like an actress feigning distress.

'You okay?' I say. 'Have you got a temperature?'

'Yes – a bloody low one!' she says. 'My hand is stuck to my forehead. And why are you talking to me like a goldfish?'

Enough was enough!

'You can stay here if you want,' says Debbie, who'd been pushing to move upstairs since October. 'I'm sleeping somewhere warmer.'

I didn't want. But with B&B demand from the Creamery running high, I was reluctant to take over one of the main guest rooms, and we moved into Ron's as soon as he left. There we would remain until the extension was built and we got our own space.

Not overlooked at the back, I nip out for Debbie's eye drops in dressing gown and slippers. I'm rarely out at this time. I can just pick out the tips of the Stiperstones above a mist hanging on the fields, and from somewhere across the brook comes the sound of Geoff's Friesians tearing at the long grass by the hedge. I feel moved in a way I don't normally afford time for, and stop to take it all in – feeling privileged to be here.

The concrete path peters into gravel at the start of the car park. I hear a rustle from one of the cars, reminding me there's a dog in the Astra –

called Bite. I'm not in view and not on the gravel; but I know what will happen when I am.

Only one thing for it – stealth. I lie on my front like a Red Indian and stalk slowly forward, pulling my dressing gown back down after each movement. Five minutes pass and Bite has no idea I'm below his car.

After another five, I reach the target and slowly move my hand to find – nothing. I try the other pocket. Nothing! Looking back, I see my car keys on the gravel where the stalking started.

'You'm playing Red Indians!' says a sharp voice nearby. 'Ha! Didna have you down as a stalker!'

All hell's let loose. If Jack made me jump, it's nothing to what comes from the Astra. Bite, a calf-high mongrel who barks beyond his weight, greets the entire neighbourhood. Mixing rapid woofing and Arctic howling with the grisly slavering of rabid lions dissecting an antelope carcass, he hurls his barrelled body at the car window.

I jump up and rearrange myself, trying to act normal, but wish I'd stayed down when I see John peering from behind a curtain at Tollgate House and Violet waving frantically from her kitchen lookout. Is it something about my dressing gown, or is she cross with Jack for being late back from his walk?

'I needed some eye drops,' I say.

'You wunna find any down there,' he says, scuffing at the gravel with his boots. 'You'll be needing the chemist in Pontesbury. They'm not open till tomorrow.'

'I'd better go inside,' I say.

'Aar' he says, like the noise you make when a doctor says, 'say aar.'

They all say that round here. The locals, I mean, not the doctors, although **they** probably do as well.

'What was all that about?' asks Debbie, taking my hard-won offering.

'Dog caught me stalking.'

'Eh? I thought I heard Jack?'

'Nah, just the dog going "Aar".'

Most dogs stay indoors, and we rely on their owners to respect the cottage. But one person's idea of respect is different from another's.

A woman from the Barbour Brigade, having walked her lurcher down Geoff's muddy farm track in pouring rain, thoughtfully wipes its feet with an old towel before stepping inside the cottage.

'He's very well behaved,' she says, as I greet her in the entrance hall.

'Madam, if I had a pound for every dog owner who says that.'

The lurcher decides now is a good time to clear his coat of itchy wet, and shakes himself vigorously until the Dulux walls that were off-white become even off-er.

Barbour doesn't even notice.

But it's a wiry whippet that provides the greatest challenge to our pets policy. Lester is led in by a middle-aged man and his mother, a sluggish woman whose thinning hair is too black.

'Can I bring you tea or coffee in the morning?' I ask, showing them into the Tulip Room.

The room is done out beautifully. Tasteful furnishings, hand-made curtains to match the wallpaper, and crocheted white bedspreads from Tenerife on each bed.

'Yes,' says the staring son, without much enthusiasm.

They seem to like the room, and their youngster certainly shows his approval, rushing around excitedly. But I can't help fearing for the bedspreads. I picture Lester galloping across them, his paws tearing through the fine fabric and depositing muddy pad marks from the brook.

'I'd prefer it if you didn't let the dog on the beds, please. As you can see, the covers are quite delicate.'

'That's all right,' says the woman, vacantly. 'He likes his own little bed. I'll put it on the floor.'

Next morning I knock lightly on the door and gently raise the latch.

'Morning,' I whisper, trying not to be too jolly first thing. 'I've got your tea.'

The scene is restful in the half dark. No-one stirs, so I edge towards the table by the double bed.

'Shall I leave it here then?'

I expect the mound in the bed to say something, and sure enough a head emerges from under the duvet. Wide-eyed and upright, head swivelling from side to side like a meerkat patrolling its hillock, Lester addresses me.

'That's fine,' he says. 'But where's mine? I only see two mugs.'

His look of disdain brands me the country oik that I am.

'Close the door quietly, will you? We won't be down for breakfast yet.'

Obediently I leave the room, turning to see Lester pat the duvet around him and lean over to count the garibaldis.

'Madam, what exactly is it you don't understand about whippets and beds?'

··· Latin Lovers ···

Aside from his stash of building materials, Jack is an inveterate collector of, well, anything. 'Don't throw it away – you never know.' The same thinking as women buying plants:

'There's no room. Where are you going to put it?'

'I'll find somewhere.'

Or shoes, come to think of it:

'You've got a hundred and fifty pairs already.'

'You can never have enough shoes.'

So Jack takes the giant pampas grass I remove from the middle of the lawn – and finds somewhere for it.

Jack takes the six young conifers outside the back door, which would soon have obliterated our view and forced us to keep the lights on all day – and finds somewhere for them.

Jack takes the turf we remove extending our garden borders, enough to lay a playing field – and makes a playing field somewhere.

And when I start demolishing the barn to make way for the extension I'm sure Jack's eyes will light up with anticipation.

I like the barn and its history. Even though we need more living space I'll be sad to see it go. Almost the same size as the cottage itself, it was built in the 1930's when the property was run as a smallholding, farming several fields nearby. In pencil, on a yellowed but intact News Chronicle I'd found hidden in the walls was written:

This cowshed was erected by LJ Sayce in November 1934

Jack says there'd also been a Dutch barn and a dairy on the site. The line where the dairy joined the back of the cottage is still visible, and the steep stone steps I've unearthed in the bank would have been used to collect brook water for cleaning it out. I cunningly christen them "The Dairy Steps".

The well we find under a manhole cover in the back path adds to the pastimes feel. Built by travelling Irish navvies (so Jack says), the neatly overlapping bricks form a perfect circle down to the scary, black water. Had it been today Debbie could have worked alongside them, pointing the bricks or taking down fresh supplies of mortar – another nice little earner. Now an historic feature in pristine condition, I could add a kitsch roof and winding bucket and call it a wishing well – suggested donation fifty pence. All for charity. Of course.

Once cleaned up, the main beams in the barn will be sound enough to use cosmetically in the ceiling of the new guest bedroom. Some of the doors, including two stable-doors, can also be recycled to marry old with new in the extension. Sadly, some features will be lost forever. A stone cow-feeding trough made by curving the concrete floor upwards along one wall of the barn will get broken up, as will two well-crafted stalls with tethering posts and iron tie-rings where horses were kept. What I can't use as cottage features will go to Jack – he'll find somewhere for them.

Jack and I often chat at the front gate or when he slips out from behind the giant screen to check something, usually because Gladys has sent him. We rarely socialise away from the cottage, but one day we go for a pint at the tiny pub he uses in the middle of nowhere – the Barley Mow at Aston Rogers.

It's not advertised, and although newcomers are made welcome the owners seem happy with their regular trade. You wouldn't find it unless someone told you. But once you're getting close, a high-pitched whine like an underpowered fifty cc moped on a long incline leads you the final few yards. This is no mechanical or electrical noise. The sages in this remote outpost talk at twice the speed of and three octaves higher than Roy of the Range Rovers, as if their noses are pegged and pants too tight. Conversations merge into a single siren that guides in new arrivals.

The seating in the square room is a wooden bench attached to the perimeter wall, the tables scrubbed pine and ring-marked from drinks gone by. A dozen or so old boys – distinctly Evanesque – are scattered along the bench in cloth caps and collarless shirts, drinking pint jugs of cheap wallop poured straight from a wooden barrel.

'Mimic spit stricter venit,' squeals a man from across the room, as Jack and I clink glasses.

'Aar,' says Jack, waving a regal hand in the man's direction. This seems to satisfy Tightpants who grins and nods – in a worrying sort of way.

The words sound vaguely Latin, so I try recalling classic words from O-level. "Venit" – maybe "glad you could come" or something? With few incomers to influence the dialect and the locals not venturing out much, maybe they've stuck with the language imposed when Romans mined lead in The Stiperstones. Or perhaps it's the lead itself having this effect, like inhaling helium gas. Although mining ceased in late-Victorian times, white spoil heaps still litter the area, their poisonous residue defying attempts at colonisation by silver birch or sycamore.

'Lick plymth necks bess fillet,' calls another man. Football? Plymouth Argyle perhaps? Rather a long way. Or beef cattle? Could be, round here.

'Aar,' says Jack, fielding people's calls with a nod and a single word. You have to be well-known and well-liked to get away with that.

The man on my other side is falling asleep. His head drops slowly forward, then jerks upright before resuming its downward trajectory. Jack says it's a family trait, that it's not falling asleep but a muscular thing. I see others doing the same, most with standy-out eyebrows, like Groucho Marx but joined in the middle. Perhaps they're related.

I decide to adopt Jack's strategy, raising an arm palm outwards to people around the room. The effect isn't quite the same but I get a few encouraging grins.

'Swiff happy kenny better,' says my nodding neighbour, jerking upright and swivelling towards me in one alarming move.

'Aar,' I reply. He bursts into laughter, making me feel strangely welcome. In a cross between Latin and Brighton we chat on and off – on when his head is up, off when it's down. I got Grade 1 for Latin O-level; at last it's coming in handy.

One of the few remaining licensed premises operating from someone's back room, you'd hardly know The Barley Mow was a pub. No frills, no pretence, and a tiny serving hatch through which the husband and wife team poke their heads to serve. Expecting the landlord to be as ancient and crusty as the pub, I'm surprised to find it run by two young teachers as a part-time hobby. How refreshing to discover such a wonderful piece of history tucked in the middle of nowhere, untouched by Beefeater and Brewers Fayre.

After a few pints, and in Jack's case cigarettes, we head home in his tidy Volvo saloon. The smell of polish and leather screams "important and successful". We've enjoyed chatting, and I've had a glimpse of Jack's social life. I feel warm and respectful towards him – even if it was all a bit strange.

'Dunna tell 'er I smoke, will you?'

'Why?'

'She'd kill me. She dunna know. I said I wunna.'

The grin on his ruddy face says he doesn't really care. It would take more than a few illicit fags to weaken his bond with Violet.

'Nightcap for me,' he says. 'Always have a little whisky. Helps me sleep.'
'Goodnight Jack. Thanks for taking me.'
'Aar.'

⋯ Minsterley – a Urinal ⋯

There are no public toilets in Minsterley. Well, that's not quite true. Tucked away near the roundabout is the Victorian Minsterley Urinal, listed by English Heritage as:

> *Grade VI Urinal. Probably late C19. Painted cast iron panels. 2 stalls with returns and central divider. Circular corner shafts, panels with pierced geometrical patterns, and moulded top rail with cresting and central dog 'gargoyle' to front. Each plate inscribed: "PLEASE ADJUST YOUR DRESS BEFORE LEAVING".*

Few such urinals have survived, but similar open-air artefacts can be found in Beverley, Yorkshire and under Moor Street Station in Birmingham. With a moulded cast-iron panel the dominant feature, they seem more common abroad, for example in France and Belgium where privacy and comfort haven't always been a priority.

The Minsterley Urinal is barely visible through a narrow entrance between stone walls. Inside, running the length of the panel, is a rough trough incorporated in the floor. The contents drain away naturally, filtered by soil and gravel before entering Minsterley Brook as relatively pure water – or that's the theory.

In autumn, open to the elements and surrounded by deciduous trees, the floor fills with leaves to a depth of five or six inches, making the position of the trough unclear. Random splattering and sloshing through leaves in the dark can be a damp and untidy affair.

There's no signpost for the Urinal. It's historically significant but of little interest to locals or tourists. Still usable, it's rarely used. Though hidden by the screen, there's a sense of exposure, like peeing in a remote, wooded area yet still glancing round nervously in case a gang of scouts comes hurtling through the brush. On exit, the trick is to wait till you hear no cars or footsteps, then emerge brisk and confident as if leaving through your own front door.

One Friday night I visit the Urinal after a few pints in town. The last bus from Shroosbury ends at Minsterley, and though I could use a pub loo to get comfortable before walking the final mile, it might be risky after my ordeal with a gaggle of women passengers.

No sooner have we left Shroosbury bus station than a middle-aged woman with a downy upper lip and three inch microskirt leans across the aisle.

'You'm up the B&B,' she says.

'Aar,' I say non-committally.

'Ee'm up the B&B,' she says to her friend in the seat behind, who passes it on to the women in the next seat back. The news about where I live filters up the opposite side of the bus, along the rear bench, and back down towards me. The smudged face of a woman past fifty appears between my headrests as if awaiting the guillotine. Her last words are:

'You'm up the B&B.'

There are more miniskirts and stilettos in this hen outing than a man of forty-two should have to cope with. Apart from a bloke at the front with an anorak wisely pulled over his ears, I'm the only man – a sitting duck for late night Minsterley predators.

'Wouldn't mind if I did!' says the downy one, staring into my eyes with a six-gin grin. 'You'm all right.'

'Aar,' I say.

'Wa-ha-ha-ha-ha!' she goes, the sort of throaty laugh I expect from blokes who start off with little sense, drink themselves senseless, then tell nonsensical jokes with "Wa-ha-ha-ha!" after the punchline to make their senseless mates go "Wa-ha-ha-ha!" back, pretending they understand.

And that's what happens. The woman behind Downy goes, 'Wa-ha-ha-ha', falling off her seat into the aisle as she loses control, and the rest of the party show their approval of what Downy "wouldn't mind if she did" by echoing the raucous laughter.

'Wa-ha-ha-ha!'

'Wa-ha-ha!'

'Wa-ha-ha-ha-ha-ha!'

Like a car that won't start. Up one side of the bus, down my side, and back the way it came.

Tired of being the butt of their masculine mirth, I play them at their own game.

'Lick belly ferry wank,' I say in a high pitch, adding 'Aar' for good measure and winking with a sideways twitch of the head. The bus goes quiet, the women looking at me and each other, unsure what to do. Downy, six-gins-ambitious, breaks the silence.

'What's that?' she says, tentatively.

'Aston Rogers – Latin,' I explain.

A smile of recognition lightens her face and the microskirt slips up beyond the legal definition of micro.

She pauses for thought, then explains to the others.

'It's Aston. Aston Rogers!' she shouts with delight. 'Ee'm Latin!'

'We thought you'm from London,' says a woman with piggy eyes.

'No, ee'm Latin,' says Downy, wriggling in her seat. 'Even better! Wouldn't mind if I did with a Latin!'

The bus arrives at the BBC stop in the nick of time. It seems unwise to use a pub loo where Downy might track me down to demonstrate exactly what she wouldn't mind doing. As they head for the Crown and Sceptre and I turn towards Minsterley Urinal, their parting shots hurry me along.

'Aar, you'm up the B&B,' calls Piggy Eyes, not realising we've dealt with that.

'Got summat special for me, Aston? Summat Latin?' yells Downy, a thought that resounds through my beery brain on the walk home – like a song you can't get out of your head.

But first the Urinal. Once through the entrance it's as dark as MOJO at midday. Having felt my way round one end of the free-standing panel, like a blind man using the moulding as Braille, I aim downwards and let gravity do the rest. Even six-pints-bold I peer through the blackness and listen, head cocked like a thrush tracking a worm.

On the few occasions I've used the Urinal I've never been joined by anyone, but now, in the stillness of the night, comes the heavy panting of someone feeling their way round the panel, like an animal nosing outside your tent before dawn. Nowhere near finished, I'm torn between staying for a predictable "at the urinal" chat and making a run for it round the other end. Nature dictates that I stay.

'Is'na easy to find 'im in here,' says a familiar voice from the other end of the trough.

'Hm,' I say, hoping to discourage further commentary.

'I know ee'm 'ere somewhere.'

Adjusting to the dark, I can see his white vest and braces and the silhouette of a cap against the night sky.

'Hello Evan,' I say, resigning myself to banal toilet talk. Having just escaped the amorous intent of the Minsterley Latin Fan Club, I'm determined not to be caught out by him too.

'Ello mate. Ow are you?' he says.

'Fine thanks. Fancy meeting you here. So this is where the big knobs hang out, Evan?'

'Aar, I heard that about *you*,' he says. 'Down London – hung like Africans, they say.'

'I thought that was the Welsh? Brighton actually.'

'It's the width that counts, boy, never mind the length.'

'Don't you mean the quality?'

'Oh, ee'm quality all right, mark my word. See you've been with them Minsterley girls.'

'What do you mean?'

'Chatting up the one with the moustache. Mate of my Mrs, she is.'

'I wasn't chatting her up. It was the other way round actually.'

'All right boy. I won't say nothing.'

'Well, there *is* nothing to say,' I tell him, rather hurriedly.

'Aar, ee'm in 'ere somewhere,' says Evan, still ferreting around in his voluminous baggies. 'Summat wrong with me buttons.'

It's nice being confided in as a genuine local, but I'd rather not hang around to help Evan with his trouser fly, let alone listen to the squelch of his slippers on the slimy concrete.

'Always mucky at the back end,' he says.

'Eh?'

'The leaves – in November.'

'Right.'

'Aar, 'ere ee be,' he says, as I go to leave. He must have loosened his braces and lowered the buttons to where they're needed.

'Got 'im goin' now.'

'Jolly good,' I call back, my initial high spirit dampened by Evan's insinuation. I exit swiftly, consoling myself with the thought that "adjusting your dress before leaving" would be a nightmare for someone like Evan – in a Victorian Urinal in the dark.

··· John Fothergill ···

I revel in the "My Basil" tag Debbie has given me. For my birthday she buys an old paperback from Quarry Books, a classy second-hand bookshop tucked off Shroosbury town centre. Inside *An Innkeepers Diary* by John Fothergill, she inscribes:

> *February 1990*
> *To My Basil.*
> *May the Fawlty within find happiness without, and*
> *may customers cherish him as much as I do.*
> *Love Debbie.*

Uncannily like Basil Fawlty, yet very much *from* the educated classes rather than aspiring to them, Fothergill had taken over The Spreadeagle Hotel in Thame, Oxfordshire at the age of forty-six, and over his ten year tenure turned it round to his liking. Set in the 1920s, it could equally have been Fawlty in the 70s or me in the 90s, such were the common themes. Understandably Fothergill resented people trying to bring in their own food or drink, but his pet hate was people coming in just to use his toilets, which he would always accost them about afterwards.

'Have you had *everything* you want? It was only a thank you *I* was wanting,' he said to one lady in the car park.

Like Fawlty, Fothergill was unable to cloak his feelings about the hoi-polloi. In his pursuit of excellence, he was anxious to expel 'vulgar boarders' and spent his first few years seeing off freemasons, farmers, 'bar people', charabanc outings and commercial travellers, or 'commercials' as he called them. Of the latter, he said:

'The poor devils are taught to shake hands on arrival as one of the means of ingratiating themselves. Some had very big and damp hands.'

And recounting a charabanc outing:

'Sixty charabanc men we had for 'dinner' from the East End. I saw their horrid charabanc coming along the clean and empty Sunday street, swoop down upon us and pull up. The sixty strong, great burly, black broad cloth-suited brutes with buttonholes all the same coloured target, leapt out.'

In stark contrast to the opinion Sybil Fawlty and I shared about filling the rooms regardless of who the customers were (barring winos), Fothergill was determined to have only 'intelligent, beautiful or well-bred people', even if it meant losing business. 'Although barely paying our way, we've declined dozens of applications for rooms, simply because we don't know the people, or the writing or the address don't please.'

Whilst these sorts of issues didn't affect me, there was a familiarity about the manner in which Fothergill dealt with people. What a birthday present! It was clear the F word would bring my performance under even closer scrutiny. Fawlty, Fothergill – Fun.

··· Downy ···

Jack and his harem never impose themselves. Okay, the giant screen is an intrusion, and B&B guests looking round the garden express surprise that the bungalow isn't part of our property. But the window was there before we came – and Jack does look after us.

He shows me how to build stone retaining walls in the garden, and along the brook to combat erosion.

He patches up the damaged lathe and plaster on the old landing walls.

He shows me tricks for starting bonfires.

He advises me on chopping and storing the surplus conifers Geoff helped take down at one end of the garden.

And he takes a genuine interest in the extension we own up to once the Planning Notice appears on the front gate.

Sadly, our bond with this wonderful countryman was soon to be lost. He'd stopped his daily bike ride and we'd noticed him taking fewer, less spritely walks round the lanes. And even though his wheelbarrow still went everywhere with him like an identical twin, it travelled more slowly and with many rests. It was a shock to find he had incurable stomach cancer and only months to live, but to the end Jack never lost his jolly smile and sense of fun. One day, as I walk out of Minsterley Post Office Stores, I hear a familiar voice.

'Hello, Latin boy.'

'I hope that's not . . .' I think, with a sinking feeling. Had she not given herself away with the L word, I wouldn't have recognised her. Wearing a full length, blue denim skirt and light cord jacket, Downy is re-arranging posters inside the glass-fronted Parish Notice Board.

'What you up to?' she says, smiling a lot less leerily than I remember from our previous encounter.

'Just needed a few things,' I say. 'They're nice, those new Post Office people.'

'Aar, Keith's a good bloke. You busy up the road?'

'Yeah, got a few in this weekend.'

Downy's demeanour is a revelation after the late-night bus episode. My strongest memories were the microskirt and what she wouldn't mind if she did to me. I'd sunk enough pints of Banks's to play along with the whims of a busload of tipsy women, bearing in mind that my own woman was sitting at home. But now I'm faced by a pleasant, well-dressed lady, seemingly not on heat.

'What were all that Latin stuff?' she says. 'You'm not really Latin, are you?'

'No!' I say, chuckling. 'That was a misunderstanding. It was the way people talked in a pub I went to. Made me think of Latin – you know, the language.'

'Can't say as I do. Which pub?' she says, standing back to check the notices are ship-shape.

'The Barley Mow over at Aston Rogers. I found their accent hard to follow – different from the one around here.'

'O-oh, you dunna wanna take n' notice of them. They'm not right. Funny eyebrows – did you notice?'

'They were very friendly. Just hard to understand.'

'Aar.'

'And some of them had this jerky neck movement,' I say, mimicking the man who'd sat next to me. 'Jack said it was a family thing.'

'That what he told you?' says Downy, laughing. 'He'm having you on. They'll have been hung over, if I'm not mistaken. Didna know Jack went there.'

'Every week, I think. It's his little retreat. He wanted to show me. I'm glad I managed to go with him – considering . . .'

'Aar, I hear he's not good.'

'No, 'fraid not. It's a shame – he's a really good neighbour.'

'He's always been pop'lar in the village. Not many as doesn't know Jack. Not much to be done, so they say.'

'No. We're trying to help Violet though. Shopping and the like.'

Downy finishes her tidying, and closes the wooden door.

'Do you do this for the Parish Council?' I ask.

'No-oo. I was making room for the W. I. posters. We've got a man from the Plant Council doing a talk; them as run the National Plant Collections – you know. You could have a poster for the B&B – your visitors can come if they want.'

'Sure,' I say. 'Debbie might be interested too. We've done a lot to our own garden – might open it to the public in a year or two.'

It's flattering how Downy takes a proper interest in what I do and I'm taken aback by her involvement with the W. I.

'My name's Carol, by the way,' she says, handing me a poster. 'Dare say you had some other names for me on the bus?'

'Not at all. But I did wonder what was going on,' I say, feeling awkward about my earlier judgement and glad to reconcile any differences.

'We'd been to see the Chippendales at the Buttermarket. Betty's fortieth.'

'Ah, that might explain it! But we had a laugh, didn't we? I'm Paul – nice meeting you too.'

'See you again, Paul,' says Downy, as we go opposite ways.

'Bye, Carol,' I say. Then as an afterthought, while she's still in earshot, 'Wouldn't mind if I did, ha ha!'

··· Pussy in the Trenches ···

Jack would love to have seen the extension built. He'd been advising me how to demolish the barn, though there isn't a lot you can teach about knocking down a building trying hard to do so by itself. A crowbar, sledgehammer and a tightrope walker's balancing pole for the top beam were all I needed. And brute force.

Sadly, he didn't live to see the first blows struck. But unable to eat and confined to his bed, he'd still listen intently to how our plans were coming along. His bony hand would grip hold of mine as if we'd known each other for years, and even when he became too sedated to talk, the glint in his eye told me he liked what we were up to. Debbie took Violet to buy him a lamb's-fleece under-blanket and other treats to make him more comfortable, and we offered her and Gladys what neighbourly support we could. Selfishly, I thought it unfair I should be deprived of such a wonderful neighbour so soon.

The crowd in Shroosbury Crematorium spilled a hundred yards from the chapel door, the service relayed through loudspeakers. And Violet, who must now care single-handedly for Gladys, whose poor circulation had been making her bedbound for long periods too, misses Jack dreadfully.

John and Meg across the road also take a positive interest in our building plans. Having spent many years at a public school in Northamptonshire, he as a maths teacher, her as domestic bursar, they'd retired to the sleepy hamlet of Plox Green a year earlier.

John and I have a lot in common – old railways, gardening, and a love of nature. We sometimes walk the hills together, setting the world to rights. His extensive vegetable garden offers a seasonal alternative to Hignett's – runner beans, tomatoes and purple-sprouting shared around when too many ripen at once. In return, our garden is now mature enough to trade feverfew and oregano seedlings or chunks of geraniums outgrowing their space.

Like me, John had latched on to Jack's stock of building materials. The only time he and I fall out is after Jack dies.

'Excuse me! Would you mind putting those back,' he says, in a schoolmasterly tone, as I barrow ex-back-of-the-lorry granite cobs from one of Jack's old stashes to my own behind the shed. Already I have piles of breeze blocks, corrugated iron sheets and whatever pieces of barn timber were wormless enough to keep. It's starting to look just like Jack's. A few more bricks and an improved "Aar" and I'll be his natural successor.

'Sorry, I don't understand,' I say, feeling guilty without knowing why.

'They're for edging my vegetable patch. Take them back, please.'

'They'd be good for edging my borders. Aren't there enough for both of us?'

'No there aren't. I need them all.'

I give in quickly. His bushy, handlebar eyebrows and upright posture are imposing, and John didn't get to be Housemaster and Head of Maths without knowing how to count granite cobs and control those around him. The cobs mean more to him than me so I graciously return them. The incident is over as soon as it's begun and we stay good friends.

I told Debbie what had happened.

'Look at you both,' she says. 'You're like long-lost cousins turning up at a funeral. The ground hasn't settled on Jack's grave and you're fighting over his legacy.'

I join Richard and Martin as a labourer to work on the extension. This reduces costs and also means I can keep an eye on progress. It's great watching a whole new house rise up around me and attach itself neatly to the old one. As well as the two new en suite bedrooms (one for guests, one for us) and the single storey, conservatory-style dining room, they cleverly add en suite facilities to the Bow and Tulip Rooms. Richard also fixes hardboard panels over the Tulip Room floor to cover the floorboards they'd laid only three years earlier, which had curled up and pulled off the joists.

'Don't worry! It'll be all right,' says Richard in his confident cockney drawl.

And it all happens without mishaps. Well only a few. Our newest cat, Thomas, disappears on the day a cement truck fills the deep footings with concrete. Having seen him treat the empty trenches as a fresh hunting ground we fear the worst. We have a soft spot for Thomas. Jack found the fluffy black and white kitten wandering in his garden, and knowing that we liked cats, bequeathed him to us. Now that's what I call a *true* legacy. That night Debbie dreams about a cat-like fossil discovered in concrete casing by alien invaders in 2150 AD. Happily Thomas turns up the next day demanding love and Whiskas. No apology though; honestly, cats have no idea of the worry they cause.

And there's a debate about roof tiles. Like mushrooms in a lawn, the new roof appears overnight. Well, kind of – we were in the Algarve when it was laid, so it felt like that when we got back. At the beginning of our venture we'd decided that foreign holidays would have to be put aside indefinitely, so when Debbie gave me a home-made crossword for Christmas and the answers spelt out "Algarve, three weeks, January 14th", I was overwhelmed. For six months she'd salted away money from cleaning and babysitting to give us a much needed break – a brilliant Christmas present!

On our return, we find huge gaps between the roof tiles. If you met someone with gaps like that between all thirty-two teeth, you'd think they were out of a James Bond movie.

'Don't worry! It'll be all right,' says Richard.

'But the gaps do look too big to me. Did you have enough tiles?' I say, trying not to sound sarcastic.

Eventually they're relaid, and though small gaps remain, the building inspector is satisfied. They add character – or so Richard says.

··· The Inspector ···

We didn't spot our first hotel inspector. They always posed as customers before revealing their true identity as they were about to leave. More often than not we'd already guessed who they were, and *they* knew that *we* knew. While it was a bit of a charade, we'd play along to make the system work.

We applied to be Tourist Board rated a year after starting. Guest Accommodation, which is how we were classified, was measured in Crowns. One was the minimum level and Five the highest. The Bow and Tulip Rooms, whilst not en suite, were tastefully done out, Ron's room at the back was plain but adequate, and the shared dining room and lounge were homely.

Waiting for our accommodation to be checked and rated for the first time by the Heart of England Tourist Board (HETB) put us in a state of suspense. A tip-off from another B&B that an inspector was in the area would have helped us apply final touches, but we only knew one or two B&Bs at that stage, so the jungle drums weren't much in evidence. In any case, it would take more than a vase of fresh flowers to improve your rating, and something serious to get marked down.

Several smart businessmen had stayed, and it could have been any one of them. In the end Malcolm turned out to be a grandfatherly, pipe-smoking type, not at all what we'd expected. The Two Crowns he gave us was a good start. Any rating was useful, in that our preferred customers typically looked for accommodation through Tourist Offices, and being rated qualified us to go in official tourist brochures which were a good source of business. And Malcolm left us knowing exactly what was needed to achieve a higher rating, so we could take this into account planning the extension.

For as long as we were paid-up members of the HETB, annual inspections were automatic. We knew the anniversary of the inspection, but not exactly when it would take place. This kept us on our toes, especially when we discovered that they sometimes skipped a visit if they were short-staffed or if a property was so obviously within a Crown rating that it would only go up or down if there were major alterations or an earthquake struck.

Strangely, this part of Shropshire *is* subject to minor earthquakes. I'd always thought fault lines were only found in far off places like Japan or Turkey, but there's one on each side of The Long Mynd, part of the Shropshire Hills Area of Outstanding Natural Beauty, and on our side it runs between Pontesbury and Bishops Castle.

On 2nd April 1990 the Pontesford-Linley Fault set off a tremor of 5.1 on the Richter scale, which became known as the Bishops Castle earthquake. At first we thought nothing of it. It was like the rumble of passing milk lorries or Wake's sludge tractors grinding up the road. But as the vibration continued I went outside to see if there were thunder clouds or other obvious explanations. Jack was poorly in bed, but Violet was outside the bungalow and Gladys was staring anxiously from the giant screen, to where she'd recently been moved for a more cheerful bed-bound existence. Part of their chimney had fallen away, not surprising since it was constructed of granite cobs and cement, which don't bind well. Our cottage wasn't affected and there was only minor damage locally, though enough to give Richard and Martin extra work for several months. The earthquake was the talk of the village.

'Aar,' says Evan in the Bridge that Monday evening. 'Ee were 7.6 on the Rizla Scale.'

'Richter.'

'Aar – Rizla.'

'No, I meant – oh, it doesn't matter.'

'What dunna matter, boy?'

'Dunna matter what dunna matter,' I say, trying to make up lost ground.

'You'm talking in riddles, boy.'

'And it was 5.1 by the way.'

'Aar – depends who's measuring it, dare say. Inna much different, seven and five.'

'If we had a 7. 6 earthquake, you'd know all about it,' I say, hating myself for sounding so serious.

'I do know all about it, boy. Seen a few earthquakes, I have.'

'Have you?'

'Aar, and floods. Soon-army down the Minsterley Brook – that's what they give.'

'Who gives?'

'The Rizla lot.'

'Right. Best have another pint while we still can then.'

'Aar, very kind, mate. Banks's,' he says, shifting a nearly empty pint towards me. 'Generous folk, these Londoners, like,' he says, turning to the man next to him.

'Aar,' says the man, looking at his glass to see whether a half might just fit in.

Gossip being transitory, when one of Wake's tractors went into a ditch a fortnight later, fracturing its tanker and spreading a field's worth of yoghurt sludge over someone's neat privet hedge, the earthquake became old news.

As 1990 wore on, we knew it would soon be time for our second inspection. There'd been several false starts.

'I'm pretty sure it's him,' I tell Debbie, having shown a smooth-suited man to the Bow Room.

'He still hasn't said anything,' she says, after taking him the bill the next morning.

Even though she wasn't usually needed, Debbie would help serve breakfast if we thought there was an inspector in the cottage, and we'd do everything with extra politeness and perfect precision.

'He will when he pays,' I say. 'Mark my word.'

The man thanks us for the excellent service and leaves. This pattern kept repeating whenever a single man or woman stayed, as a result of which many guests were receiving customer service beyond their Two Crown imaginations. But still no-one owned up.

In late summer I demolish the barn, and Martin and Richard move onto the levelled site with a JCB. The car park is put over to a working area – piles of sand and gravel, pallets of cement covered with blue plastic, and giant stacks of bricks and breeze-blocks. As Atlantic depressions track across Plox Green for three weeks, puddles of cement surround the growing edifice, with offcuts of wood and rubble ready to trip the unwary passer-by.

Between ten and four o'clock, outside the agreed noise curfew, the thud of a sledgehammer and rumble of a laden cement mixer is never far away. Dust and grime find their way into the cottage on clothing and through cracks and crevices. Thick dust sheets barely protect the floors and carpets. And as the extension gets higher, having already been forced to park their cars on the sodden grass verge opposite, guests have to skirt mucky puddles under an array of coarse scaffolding and splintered planks. I'd written to the HETB, suggesting they postpone an inspection until the work had been completed in the New Year. But of the few people who turn up in December, one suited gentleman shows every sign of being an inspector.

'Working locally?' I ask.

'Yes, just a few calls,' he says'

'Young, ambitious, cool. It must be him,' thinks My Basil.

The man follows the routine of the first inspector, lying low in the Tulip room, presumably to catch up on paperwork and avoid conversation that might give him away. The other guest, a middle-aged woman from Winchester, is visiting her elderly mother in a local care home. I admire her resolve, travelling alone in such gloomy weather, and it's good to offer her a warm winter haven. She joins us by a crackling fire to watch the Nine o'clock News. Whatever she's knitting will nicely match the chunky, marmalade cardigan draped across her sturdy frame.

At breakfast she helps distract the inspector's thoughts from the mess of construction, expressing her delight with the Bow Room before he's even had a chance to inspect it himself. Debbie and I move into overdrive, her applying feminine wile, me creating a top breakfast served at exactly the right time.

The man takes the bill to his room, whilst in the kitchen My Basil practises his response to the inspector's imminent revelation:

'Oh, really? Well I hope everything's been okay for you.'

Maybe more assertive:

'Ah, good. We'd been expecting you.'

'Thank you. A lovely breakfast,' says the man ten minutes later, handing over his cash. 'And the room was very comfortable.'

'Now we're talking! Come on – feed me the line.'

'Oh, good,' I say.

'How long will the construction work last?'

'Well, I did tell the Heart of England tourist Board,' I say, pre-empting the inevitable criticism.

'It's not a problem,' he says. 'I've got a lot of work in the area, so I'm sure I'll be back. You seem to be coping well.'

'Phew, thank goodness for that!'

'Cheerio for now,' he says, heading for the door with briefcase and holdall.

'Wait a minute! We need to discuss our rating first!'

'Er, yes, bye,' I say, flummoxed. 'Nice seeing you.'

'Bloomin' heck,' I shout to Debbie. 'It wasn't him after all.'

'Never mind,' she calls back. 'He seemed the type though.'

Behind me, ready to leave, is the marmalade lady.

'Thank you, that was very nice,' she says, cheque and guarantee card in one hand, business card in the other. 'I'm from the Tourist Board. Do you have a moment to talk about your rating?'

In the lounge, Debbie and I glance at each other nervously, trying to recall what Betty Caldicott might have overheard or seen us doing.

'It's not ideal entering through muddy pools under scaffolding,' she says. 'Understandable, yes, but I do have to assess you on what I find.'

Fair enough. Clearly she can't yet promote us from Two Crowns, and we're grateful the mess hasn't in fact lowered our rating. After looking through the building plans – a third en suite guest bedroom, the Sun Room for dining, and a crisp new car park – Betty says that, with fresh decorations inside and out, we'll be certain of Four Crowns. Better still, she offers to re-inspect in the spring to confirm the rating.

And she really *was* visiting her mother, doubling business with a social trip. Thanks, Miss Marmalade. We love your cardigan, and you're *so* much nicer than that young man. We thought he was a bit glib actually.

⋯ Cutting It Out ⋯

We have ourselves a brand new cottage! The building site has disappeared, we're assured of a Four Crown rating, and foreign holidays are back. A great time to decide what other changes to ring. Our "welcome all" attitude had been important for getting established, but we knew there'd be decisions to make as the Bed and Breakfast grew.

There were several plump targets. The first and easiest was smoking. Debbie had never smoked and I'd given up fifteen years earlier. Compared with the 60s and 70s, smokers were in the minority, and visitors increasingly looked for smoke-free environments. We were confident that banning smoking would attract more guests in the long run.

The greatest gain is at mealtimes. In the old dining room guests had to share a large table. This was never ideal. Conversation, hard enough first thing in the morning, was already forced, and it only took one smoker for the atmosphere to deteriorate further – in more ways than one.

Now that dining is in the Sun Room, with separate tables and background radio, the atmosphere is relaxed, the air clear. Given their own space, people chat more freely. Views of the garden and the Stiperstones Ridge make good ice-breaking topics, so that easy conversation starts across tables too. And we find that those who *do* smoke are happy to go outside rather than not stay at all. Our judgement had been well founded.

But there are still those who think that "going outside" means puffing from a bedroom window and letting the smoke drift back in. Probably the same ones who furtively drop dog-ends from the window thinking they'll magically disappear and not clog my gutters or leach toxic chemicals into the garden for ten years.

And there are those who don't view the garden as a warm, colourful paradise, but the perfect place to dump their detritus. Thank goodness for the thoughtful folk who wouldn't dream of trashing the flower borders, but instead flick their butts on the car park.

Oh, and I nearly forgot those who smoke so heavily that on entering the room they give off an acrid smell second only to chicken shit.

'They say ex-smokers are obsessively self-righteous,' says Debbie.

'So I heard,' I say. 'Must be awful to get like that. At least we still let them smoke outside; down the Hanwood B&B they've banned smoking anywhere on their land.'

The next target was pets. Goldfish had been generally quiet, and stick insects didn't rush about much. And no noisy parrots had turned up. But dogs had proved more difficult. We had nothing as such against canine company, but in public people and dogs didn't always go. If they'd all been temperament-tested, like the wonderful dogs and cats supplied by the Pets as Therapy (PAT) charity for visits to hospitals and care homes, they'd be welcome. But for every spaniel that uses its own bed we get a whippet that prefers sleeping with women; for every shy chihuahua, a mongrel who wants to eat everyone up; for every dog lover, a guest who isn't. And for every well-behaved PAT type, there's one that wants to jump up and slobber or rub itself to delirium on my rush matting or someone's lower leg.

'He's only being friendly,' the owner would say.

'Madam – if I was friendly towards you like that, I'd be locked up. So if you wouldn't mind.'

Dogs can still be left in the car. It just means that everyone has to be on Bite-alert if they need anything outside after dark; tip-toeing on the gravel, hunched up in dressing gowns. And having cats is an added complication since cats and dogs take a while getting used to each other. Cats have always been a part of our household, but we confine Oliver and Thomas to our own living area, not just when there are dogs around but in case guests have an aversion to them. People with allergies usually ask about pets in advance.

Only the worst sufferers fail to come, but we're caught out once – by a rare case of felinophobia. At breakfast something on one of the tables seems wrong; I notice the place mats have changed colour.

'Everything okay?' I say.

'Yes, fine.'

'Is there a problem with the mats?'

'Len doesn't like cats,' says his wife, since the stocky man with swarthy beard and lumberjack's shirt is clearly too stressed to speak for himself. 'So we turned them over.'

The cats on the mats are an artist's impression, in the same style as Kings and Queens on playing cards. Harmless to most but a nightmare for Len.

'Would you like me to change them?' I ask him.

'No, don't worry,' his wife replies. 'As long as he can't see them.'

'Well watch out, Lenny, because that Siamese will JUMP out from under the mat as soon as it smells your bacon!'

The third change was children. Debbie is good with children, me less so. We both get on well with young nephews and nieces when they come to stay, but with them we have an element of control; with guests' children we don't.

After Earth Mother, My Basil had put up a notice saying:

> *Nappy changing and breast feeding permitted in the living room, but please note it means I shall serve breakfast naked*

That did the trick, but it didn't really cover toddlers. At six one morning I emerge from a dream about cowboys at the O.K. Corall to find that the horses' hooves are on the landing corridor, where the parents have released their two under-fives from the Tulip room to play tag. I leave them to it. Intervening would cause even more disturbance, and I imagine the romantic couple in the Bow Room next door were already happy with one early morning call.

Another time, Debbie asks a woman in the living room about the noise from upstairs.

'Are your children all right on their own?' she asks.

'They're just playing,' says the exhausted woman, spinning out her respite.

'Only I'm a bit worried about the china.'

'They're very good,' she says, as the rumpus permeates through the cottage. 'I've told them not to touch anything.'

'I'd rather you checked. There are some fine antique ... make that "were" ', says Debbie, shoving past the woman towards the sound of crunching drip-glaze vases, aged sixty, dying before their time. Children's playtime comes to an abrupt end.

My dad also found it too much on one occasion. Both sets of parents had taken to coming up from Brighton once or twice a year. Mine liked popping into Shroosbury or driving round the Welsh Borders by day, and taking us to the local pubs for dinner. They loved the area, treating the cottage as a second home. No doubt they were still concerned with my financial wellbeing, and their generosity was certainly welcome – no tent for them! But I think the D word was now okay; they were quietly noting my success and getting my Drift.

The Stables Inn and the Yockleton Arms were two of their favourite places. At the remote seventeenth century Stables Inn at Hopesgate, originally a drovers' pub, the well-spoken and businesslike landlord Denis keeps a cracking pint of Shropshire Lad, flagship beer of the small Wood brewery attached to the Plough Inn at Wistanstow, near Craven Arms. And his rarely-seen wife Debbie makes a pretty good boeuf bourguignon and an immaculate pork loin in creamy mustard sauce. The bistro-style dining area encourages you to linger, and the log fire in the bar is perfect for a pre-prandial pint and a little something to round off the meal.

Bed and Breakfast guests speak highly of the pub, and we use it frequently if only for a few drinks. For mum and dad it was a must. There are rarely negative reports, although both Debbie and Denis, whilst producing excellent fayre, are unpredictable. Denis in particular can turn sharply on customers late in the evening when his bottomless red wine appears to take hold, and rumour has it that farm folk who frequented the bar before he came were, as at The Spreadeagle in Thame, eliminated at an early stage.

The Yockleton Arms near Worthen is much grander, the place for a special occasion or a visit from best friends or relatives. When we arrived in Shropshire it was a humdrum roadside pub called The Pink Elephant, but it's now run by four enterprising young people as a restaurant offering top class cuisine in an intimate atmosphere. A highly professional formula makes it by far the best restaurant for miles, and you don't get in without booking.

It was the morning after a Chateauneuf-du-Pape-driven night at The Yockleton that my dad found himself in the wrong place at the wrong time. No doubt feeling as proud as Clive Sinclair did in his first C5, a toddler had turned a cardboard box into a fire engine – or rather his father had – and using his feet as fuel was exploring every inch of floor space, including our living room.

It isn't the vehicle running over dad's legs that raises his blood pressure, but the loud siren that clears the way.

'Nee-nah! Nee-nah!'

'Please don't do that, you irritating boy.'

'Nee-nah! Nee-nah! Nee-nah!'

'Where's the fire,' I say, trying to distract him.

'Nee-nah! Nee-nah! Nee-nah! Nee-nah!'

Having said nothing for five minutes, my dad, a major in the Burma campaign and similar in many ways to Fawlty's Major Gowen, can tolerate it no longer.

'Stop that NOW!' he yells from the sofa. Clearly, he'd let his frustration well up, making an outburst inevitable. His idea of bringing up children didn't include noisy fire engines in public places, especially if you felt a bit fragile, and in his view the boy's parents had had ample time to do something about it.

The irritating boy, unfamiliar with this sort of request, does an emergency halt and stares at dad. At the same time his parents appear at the door. The irritated couple quickly usher the irritating boy from the irritated Costellos and quit the cottage, never to be seen again. We introduce a minimum age of eight.

No smoking, no dogs, no toddlers. Over the course of a year we at last get some of our bigger, better cottage back to ourselves.

⋯ The Fat American ⋯

Naming the new guest bedroom is easy. The colour of the paint and the Albertine climber that will soon surround the windows make Rose Room an obvious choice.

The first occupants are our good friends Tony and Anne, a couple from North London who've taken a shine to our cottage and stay two or three times a year. We're not often on first name terms with guests. Most people call us Debbie and Paul, but *they* only have two names to remember, both of which are on our brochure. We can't remember the surnames, let alone first names of everyone who stays. And it's risky trying.

'Morning Paul.'

'Morning Peter.'

'It's Phil actually.'

'Eh?'

'Phil – my name's Phil.'

'Oh yes, of course.'

Better to call everyone "There".

'Morning Paul.'

'Hello There. Sleep all right?'

'Not too bad. Cuckoos were outrageously loud though.'

'I agree – terribly noisy in the countryside. Will Mrs There be joining you for breakfast?'

Tony and Anne take a personal interest in our success, and friendship comes naturally. It's good letting them christen the Rose room, with its barn timbers, sloping ceilings and Georgian-paned windows to match the old cottage, and the privacy of its own staircase.

As summer moves on, we look back at what we've achieved in three years.

We've created, as it were, a new-old cottage, cleverly thought out, with delightful guest areas and at last our own space; trade is good, customers are returning, and we've reclaimed our home in the sense of choosing who stays; the neighbours are lovely, though we miss Jack; the garden is blossoming and almost fit for opening to the public; we've had winter warmth, strolling the beaches of Albufeira by day and supping Sagres beer by night; Debbie has a new job with English Heritage at Haughmond Abbey, near Shroosbury, and I'm running a top quality B&B. Life is good.

And then a fat American breaks my bed.

Debbie reckons I pick on Americans. But I say what I see. If it were a German, I'd tell it the same but add something about ruthless efficiency and lack of humour. Or for Turks, disrespect.

Americans are a small and highly volatile part of my trade. Ever since the tragic destruction of Pan Am Flight 103 over Lockerbie in 1988, it had taken only a whiff of insecurity, such as a report that a mixed-race man was found with a children's tea set in his suitcase, for Americans to shy away from international travel. A major crisis like the Gulf War at the start of 1991 guarantees wholesale boycott. And of course, Americans' unwillingness to travel means the whole of America loses out. Not only do the travellers fail to see the wonders of the world, but the rest of The States has to put up with them staying over there.

Some are okay. The hippy, free-love and flower-power couple from California who thought we were "Heaven-on-Earth" wouldn't be put off. But Americans from the Eastern seaboard are more security conscious, and those that do come are more demanding.

'Had trouble getting out of Edinburgh,' says a large man, explaining a later than expected arrival.

'You've not done badly,' I say. 'It's a long way.'

'Sure is. Didn't leave much time for York and the Lake District. We like an hour at those places.'

'An hour's not much for the Lake District,' I say.

'Nothing there, so we moved on.'

'You can take that one first,' his scrawny woman tells me, pointing at one of several huge cases in the boot.

'Wait! I'm talking to your fat husband!'

I say hello to their friends in the other car, both of whom are larger than the first man. Three fat people, a scrawny one, ten large cases, and two giant rental cars to haul them around.

I wonder if the scrawny one is of Oriental origin. But when the others chuckle at something and she doesn't react, I realise her face has been lifted so much that she is saddled with a fixed grin between the earlobes, like say, an estate agent's grimace before telling a lie. Tampering with her neck has made the head disappear into the shoulders, and hollows are left where her cheeks have been pulled off their axis. A rolling teardrop would now hit an unexpected void like a ha-ha in the grounds of a country house. And because the cheeks are where the eyes should be, it leaves only the tiniest slits to peep out from.

Her scrawniness is harder to explain – for an American. Perhaps she was once fat like the others, before being liposucked to her present size, possibly at the same time as her face was moved around.

'I'll take this one then come back for the other nine,' I say.

'That's okay,' says Scrawny. 'Leave the small one. My husband can manage that.'

'Thanks, that's very kind,' I say.

They want every item of luggage taken inside overnight – for security. If Bite had been in the car park, he could have guarded them. After twenty minutes I'm shattered.

'Is everything all right for you?' I ask later.

'Rooms are a bit small, but they'll do,' says the fatter of the two men.

'I think you'll find it's your obesity and the cases.'

'Tell me, do you get hot water around here?'

'The tap marked "H", dickhead!'

'It may take a minute to come through,' I say, trying not to give away too much disdain; I'd like to hold some back for later.

For those not dining at Cricklewood, each room has sample menus of places to eat locally. I only recommend those that match the ambience of the cottage, places we'd go ourselves. The Minsterley pubs, which are the only ones within walking distance, are not included because a) they **don't** match the ambience, b) visitors might not understand the dialect when asked if they'd like mash or chips with Ye Olde Oak Ham pie, and c) they often say they do food, then don't.

But there are many tasteful inns and restaurants towards Shroosbury or tucked away in the hills. As well as the Stables and The Yockleton, guests talk fondly of the Stiperstones Inn, high up in hill-walking territory. It has a shop, Post Office, B&B, camping field and organised chaos. Open all hours, the shop is a maze of small, low-ceilinged rooms with shelves holding one of everything you could possibly want. One VO5 shampoo, one cheese grater, one set of chimney sweeping brushes, one sketch map of the shop to find your way back out. MOJO eat your heart out.

The pub can be hit and miss. You may wait ages for food, only to find they've forgotten to pass your order to the chef. But it's worth the wait – traditional pub grub, plenty of it, and hard to spend more than a couple of quid.

The shy landlord John, lean from fell running, migrates between shop and pub in a faded blue tracksuit, treating everyone like a long lost relative. I imagine he's a shrewd businessman, owning four race horses as he does.

'Which restaurant do you recommend?' asks one of the fat American men, realising they are too late to eat at the cottage.

I hesitate to suggest the usual ones. None will take lightly to abuse and greed, and I want to protect my reputation. But all is not lost. I keep to one side the menu for a small cafe, tailor-made for Americans feeding a fat frenzy.

From somewhere in the interior of Utterly Undiscovered, as sluggish and persistent as a lava flow, runs a rare stream of saturated fat. An enterprising local decided to open a cafe for those with a predilection for the stuff. He tapped the stream and from the aptly named Fat Place, just inside civilisation, serves saturated fat neat, or with thick slices of white Mother's Pride bread for the extra needy.

This remains something of a secret. If it was less remote or if the locals had ventured out to spread the story, the fat would have become nationalised like other utilities and Mrs Thatcher would now be selling it off. A tempting thought, since it would have given us another windfall on top of the privatisation of gas, electricity, water and telephones.

Fat Americans to the Fat Place are like flies to Geoff's cow-pats. My full English breakfast will seem tame by comparison. Later, arteries bolstered, one of them asks:

'Do you have any poker chips?'

'Did you see a flashing "Casino" sign outside?'

Debbie and I retire to bed, wondering how wise it is to leave games out for guests, as through the still of the Shropshire night we hear the rattle of dice in a cup and the thwack of solitaire marbles being thrown into a bag – one by one . . .

They do Bath and London tomorrow before flying out at midday for an hour in Paris on the way home. Should be okay for poker chips in London or Paris. Or any chips come to that.

But it wasn't one of this party who broke my bed. That happened later in the year.

I hear the boom of approaching footsteps. When I open the door it's like dusk as the giant figure casts a shadow over the cottage.

'Hello, come in,' I say.

'If you can,' says My Basil.

Carrying a strangely small suitcase, the huge woman levers herself slowly through the doorway and down into the guests' lounge, delivering a 6.3 shock on the Richter scale. Neighbours will be rushing for cover, fearing that the Pontesford-Linley line is active again. Kimberley is as wide as she is tall – and that's tall. Her girth would dwarf Bernard Manning's, and like Bernard Manning her head sits on top like a tiny nipple, with oversized dark glasses resting precariously on the forehead. She is about twenty. And she will adore the Fat Place.

I lever her through the narrow upstairs corridor and, taking a sideways tack, she squeezes her way into the Tulip Room. I last see her heading for the garibaldis.

Thunder rolls in the distance as Kimberley turns at night. It's like Jack and the Beanstalk in your own home. 'Fee-fie-foe-fum, I hear a fat Amer-i-can.'

'She'm fat,' says Violet astutely, next day as Kimberley screeches off down the road. 'Car's tilting.'

Later, I lean across her bed to remove the linen – and collapse in a heap, just as Kimberley must have done. The thick screw in a corner leg has been ripped from its threaded socket and bent out of recognition. She has dropped on the bed with the impact of a swinging stone on a demolition crane. It didn't stand a chance. No wonder she made a quick getaway!

I'm relieved to find the toilet and shower tray watertight, and wonder if the overnight thunder had been porcelain groaning on floorboards. Today's task is to find a replacement bed in Shroosbury for tonight. Money out; my insurance doesn't cover Fat Americans.

··· Tying the Knot ···

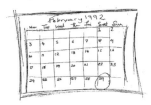

Marrying Debbie had never been top of my "must do" list. My first marriage, to Alison, had petered out after six years, and though we'd remained friends I'd felt no inclination to re-enter that most hallowed of institutions.

Debbie on the other hand hadn't experienced the delights of wedlock. In our nine years together she'd not pushed to get married, though the subject had arisen more often in the last few. Taking my name by Deed Poll had been a pretty big hint, I suppose; I'd mopped my brow and thought, 'That's all right then.'

We enjoyed sharing the cottage and building a new life together. I was proud of the B&B's success, Debbie loved her job with English Heritage, and we complemented each other about the house and garden – my practical approach and Debbie's creativity.

Sometimes these attributes clashed.

'We need Farrow and Ball paint in the Reading Room,' says Debbie. 'It'll set off the pine fittings nicely.'

Now that guests eat in the Sun Room, the old dining room has become the guests' lounge, or Reading Room as we've christened it. A Persian rug matches the quarry tile floor we found sweating under thick floral Axminster. The antique pine bookshelves – train books for men, gardening for women (it works) – and a glowing coal fire on chilly autumn evenings complete the cosy feel.

'How much is it?' I ask.

'Only ninety-eight pounds a tin. Look – this colour's perfect. Two tins should do it.'

'That's orange,' I say. 'B&Q do an orange for five pounds eighty.'

'Excuse me, that's Burnt Georgian Sienna.'

'Same thing. And the tins are only two litres. B&Q's are two point five.'

'Well I want Farrow and Ball.'

'What if we have one wall of that and the rest B&Q?'

'Why don't you stick to what you're best at? Putting the stuff on.'

'Oh, all right then.'

The outcome was nearly always for the best, but reached the long way round.

'Have you thought about us getting married?' Debbie asks one day, catching me off guard.

With that as the question, the answer was easy.

'No I haven't,' I say.

When she changed tack it got harder.

'I think we should get married.'

'Hm.'

'I said, I think we should get married.'

'Sorry, I didn't realise it was a question.'

'Well? What do you think?'

'Hm, I'd have to think about that.'

I get away with that reply until 1992 kicks in.

'Will you marry me?'

'Hm, I'd have to think about that.'

'You do realise it's a leap year?'

'So it is.'

'So – what do you say?'

'Hm, I'd have to think ––'

'What do you say?' Debbie says, firmly.

'I'd have to think about it between now and the twenty-ninth of February.'

The discussion puts us on edge, leaving a strange atmosphere about the cottage. We know something's going to happen but there's nothing to be said before the twenty-ninth. The romantic notion of a leap year engagement makes me think about marriage more seriously, and deep down I know that, having come a long way together and made it work, marrying Debbie would now be absolutely the right thing for us. I give nothing away though. After all, we have a pizza date on the twenty-ninth and I wouldn't want to spoil the occasion.

Saturday 29th February 1992 – the Sun Room. A bottle of Cabernet Sauvignon, pizzas (pepperoni and ham 'n pineapple), and safe conversation:

Her: 'Been mild today.'

Me: 'Yeah. Rain tomorrow, they say.'

Her: 'Who says?'

Me: 'Evan.'

Her: 'Pizza's nice.'

Then:

'Paul, will you marry me?'
'Hm, I'd have to --'
'Don't *do* this to me!'
'--definitely say "Yes, I will".'

Friday 27th November 1992 – Ludlow Registry Office. We've deliberately chosen a November wedding so as not to lose out on B&B. Actually – I have. And Debbie, already falling in line with the requirements of union, simply has to love, honour and obey my bookings diary.

'Do you, Paul Costello take you, Debbie Costello to be your lawful wedded wife?'

'Hm, I'd have to think . . . oh sorry, daydreaming. Yes, I do.'

Seeing the same surnames, the Celebrant does a quick eyebrow count and raises her own. She'll know we live near Utterly Undiscovered. But we'll be away before gossip spreads this side of the hills – honeymooning in Madeira.

The Algarve? Madeira? Ha! We'll be over the moon by the Millennium.

··· Key of the Door ···

Guests are given keys – for the front door and the bedroom. We like people to come and go as they please and feel secure about their room. A far remove from the 50s and 60s when you had to be out of the building by ten and stay out till four.

'We'd never give out keys,' say some of our security-minded friends. 'Doesn't it worry you?'

Thinking about it, there *is* nothing to worry about. Having decided to let strangers into your house, you've already given them the opportunity to walk out with your prize china, so keys will make no difference.

'But what if they lose them or give copies to their villainous burglar friends?'

We point out that our guests are mostly retired people, or families and young professionals, and that if they have villainous friends they aren't likely to hang around in a remote part of Shropshire on the off chance of stealing damp towels or the failing fifteen year old Panasonic TV their advance party has tipped them off about. As for losing keys – well, they're not labelled, so they could belong anywhere.

It's the townie side to our friends. We'd found country life so crime-free and safe – people looking after each other's property – that fear of violation fell away like wet snow off a roof. Even in Brighton we'd let student lodgers have keys, though arguably that had been a greater risk.

A few things *have* gone missing though. I can never understand someone taking a whole toilet roll. If they've got a cold or an upset stomach they might need a small supply for emergencies, but taking a sealed roll is theft. Though not in the same league as a Bank of England heist, it's sad that someone who likes our cottage enough to stay should be so light-fingered.

I also caught a Creamery contractor with one of our towels in his work bag. It turned out he'd gone straight from work to Shroosbury Swimming Pool; after telling him what the towels were really for, I let him off.

I did come unstuck in the first year though, when I thought a customer had walked off with a coat hanger designed by Debbie. Determined to keep my property intact, I sent the culprit a letter:

> *Dear Mrs Hook*
> *Just to say how lovely it was seeing you at Cricklewood Cottage, and you're welcome back any time.*
> *I wonder if you could help me? One of the coat hangers in your room appears to be missing. I wouldn't have worried if it was a wire one, but this is a padded hanger that matches the curtains and is part of the room furniture. Could you please check to see whether it might by chance be attached to an item of your clothing? If it does come to light I'd appreciate your returning it, but thanks for looking anyway.*

I'm halfway to Australia, excavating a sunken terrace as a place to hide from the giant screen, when the trusty cordless rings.

'Hello, I've received a letter from you – about a coat hanger,' says the lady.

'Oh yes –– '

'We did *not* take your coat hanger and how dare you suggest we *did*! Do we look like the kind of people who'd steal?'

'Well may –– '

'Do you seriously think we're that poor that we'd steal coat hangers? What kind of a place do you run?'

'Well, can I just –– '

'We liked your cottage and thought we might come back, but I don't think that's going to happen now – do you?'

'I'm ever so sorry, I had no intention of –– '

'It's a bit late now. If you think we'd ever come again, forget it. Goodbye.'

'Fine – make sure your friends don't come either!'

I'm left taking rapid breaths, wondering if I've dug a hole deep enough. I feel a fool. One coat hanger – not such a great loss, I suppose. But I love my cloth-covered country coat hangers and I'm trying to hold my household together. How dare she! Okay, I'll let her off; but if there's a run on hangers I'm going in hard.

Note to self: talk to Debbie about switching to those bland, grey hangers, where the hook doesn't come off the rail.

Such moments of naivety were commonplace in the early days. Our resolve to have things perfect was unrealistic, our enthusiasm sometimes misplaced. My chasing after the burly builders still embarrassed me, though I could now see the funny side of it. On another occasion we were clearly at fault by omission. A knock on the living room door jolts me from a nap after a hard day in the garden. It's the couple staying in the Bow Room.

'Hello, did you have a nice day?' I say.

'I'm sorry, there's a problem with our room,' the woman says, straight-faced.

'Oh, how can I help?'

'It hasn't been made up – it doesn't look as if anyone's been in there.'

I feel like crawling behind the sofa. In our enthusiasm to work on the garden we'd completely forgotten to service their room.

'I'm so sorry, I had no idea. I assumed Debbie had done it and she must have thought I had.'

'Well if you wouldn't mind . . .' she says, not at all convinced.

'Yes, of course, I'll do it now. Come in – I'll get you a drink while you're waiting.'

My charm offensive helps, and I leave them with tea and garibaldis before slinking off, rosy-faced, to make up for our elementary error. We were learning fast.

Arguably, we make up for things that go missing by keeping what people forget to take with them. Books are common; a pair of lined, leather gloves serve me well; and a young couple left a nice set of 'His and Hers' cappuccino mugs. Perhaps one in ten people forget something. To begin with we'd telephone them, offering to send stuff on, and their reaction was normally:

'Did I? Oh, I didn't realise. Yes, I suppose you could.'

Few seemed to appreciate our gesture, and since it didn't really gain us any brownie points we decided to return property only if they contacted us first. Even then there was no thought for the time and money we put into doing it, so we started asking people to refund the postage. One New Zealand tourist called about a white, pleated bowling skirt she'd left, asking if we'd post it to her home address since she was about to leave the UK – and, yes, of course she'd refund the cost. I walked out of the Post Office £5 lighter in pocket and never heard from her again. From then on we asked people to send cash or stamps in advance, or else we couldn't help them.

I never felt a conscience about this. While guests were at the cottage I gave them everything they needed. But the B&B offered a modest living, and My Basil's generosity didn't stretch to subsidising absent-minded people.

Giving keys to guests also left us free to go out ourselves or retire to bed if they were back late. This was especially useful with weddings. We were a popular stop-over for wedding guests – My Basil loved telling people about the bride-to-be who ate kippers before her wedding – and guests usually arrived at midday to get ready for the occasion, typically an afternoon wedding in a village church followed by a reception at Rowton Country Castle Hotel, a magnificent seventeenth century property just west of Shroosbury. Since they were likely to return late, a set of keys gave everyone the freedom they needed.

One time the system didn't work was when two businessmen, Gary Roberts and Sean O'Connell, stayed prior to an important management meeting at the Creamery the following day. On request, I give them an extra front door key and point them in the direction of the local pubs.

'I'll see you at breakfast, if not before,' I say.

'That'll be noice,' says Sean, glowing with Southern Irish charm. 'Oi'll look farward to that.'

Shortly after I've gone to bed I hear the front door shut, and since they're the only guests, I fall asleep knowing I won't be disturbed further.

At some time in the middle of the night I'm woken by a scratching noise, like a mouse picking over debris between the joists. The noise dies off briefly but resumes with added persistence, and I start mulling over how to catch the varmint in the morning. Debbie is fast asleep, but I'm now fully awake and irritated; after what seems like half an hour I decide to investigate.

The night lights filtering down the staircases help me creep across the Reading Room without waking the guests. The scratching doubles in volume when I open the door to the small front hall. Clearly someone is trying to break into the cottage and hasn't realised that noise magnifies at night in the country. I have no reason to think it's a mad axeman – but it might be. And through the small, frosted pane in the front door I can definitely see the outline of an intruder going about his business. For once the security chain is handy. As I peek through the gap an arm lunges towards me from the black night.

'Surry,' comes a familiar voice, a key waving in erratic circles at roughly lock height.

'Surry, coon't foind the lark,' he says, with little backwards and forwards steps and prodding hand movements. I remove the chain.

'Oi gut . . . surry. Surry, oi . . .' with which the momentum of Sean's forward sway carries him over the doorstep where I offer a helping hand to keep him steady.

'Turn right at the top and your room is straight ahead,' I say. As an afterthought I follow him up the stairs to make sure he's going the right way for the Tulip Room, where Gary must already be asleep.

It's three o' clock and I lie awake expecting unpleasant toilet noises or the thump of a ten-stone Irishman falling over. But it all goes quiet.

'I had to let your mate in last night,' I say to Gary, who sits alone at breakfast. 'Hope it didn't disturb you.'

'Nah,' he says, more London than Dublin. 'I left him at the Bridge. He's good at spotting a lock-in. I could see what was going to happen.'

'Not so good at spotting a *lock* though!' I say.

Sean enters the Sun Room, pasty-faced, and sways gently in his chair just as he had done at the front door a few hours earlier.

'What can I get you?' I ask, enjoying the moment.

'Oi'll be all roit,' he says, trying to avert his eyes from Gary's cooked breakfast. 'Oi'll just have ter juice, tanks.'

I leave them to discuss tactics for their imminent business conference.

··· Malcolm Returns ···

As well as running the B&B more to our own liking, we now have a solid Four Crowns Tourist Board rating. Or Four Diamonds to be precise – the system has changed, Diamonds replacing Crowns for Guest Accommodation, and several tourist agencies agreeing to inspect properties in the same way. The AA has joined the scheme, though the RAC wouldn't sign up, and whilst the Scottish Tourist authorities are now part of it, the Welsh declined. Fair enough – would England want to join the Welsh scheme, I wonder?

Frankly I don't care. I've seen enough reorganisations in my life to take them for what they are – something to further the career interests of the manager or politician engineering the change. (Thanks again, Slithery, by the way). The effectiveness of a new structure is hard to measure, and is often superseded by the next reorganisation before it has had a chance to mature, with the hidden costs of planning, printing, publicity and office changes rarely getting a mention.

"Diamonds" sounds good to me, and whether it covers the whole UK doesn't concern me, except perhaps when I'm travelling myself. As long as it applies to Plox Green and I'm four out of five, that'll do nicely. It can be Buffaloes or Beefburgers as far as I'm concerned. Probably is in the States.

A pleasant surprise for our 1993 inspection is the return of Malcolm. He'd been our first inspector in 1989 which meant he could see the changes we'd made and chat about our progress with genuine enthusiasm. We'd had one other inspection since Miss Marmalade returned to confirm our Four Crowns, as it then was. As usual this had been incognito – or so Jeremy thought. On that occasion we'd spotted him like a German in a line-up of comedians.

Malcolm phoned in advance and didn't stay the night. Since he knew us, and we were comfortably within the Four Diamond rating, there was no point in clandestine tactics. We simply went through the motions over coffee and biscuits.

He said he'd been given lighter work by the Tourist Board, because since we last saw him he'd had a heart attack whilst driving between inspections. Fortunately he'd realised what was happening, and had been able to pull off the busy road and get help before collapsing. Goodness knows what awful things he must have seen at the place he'd just inspected. Though fully recovered, he was kept away from stressful situations, such as trying to pretend he was someone he wasn't.

I wondered how light his work really was when he told us of an incident the previous month. He'd been sent to check complaints about a hotel in Ironbridge, whose name he couldn't give us for reasons of confidentiality, but he said, 'It sounds something like the name of the Lone Ranger's sidekick.' It seems that, amongst other bad practices, they'd been cooking large batches of sausages and storing them in the fridge for weeks on end, re-heating them as needed for breakfasts. He'd passed the matter to Environmental Health who'd suspended activity in the kitchen until further notice. The problem had been resolved, but Malcolm must have felt shaky dealing with it.

Our only concern at his inspection was whether we'd be penalised for no longer offering evening meals. When we stopped taking pets and young children, and banned smoking in the cottage, we'd shied away from the plumpest target of all. Dinners had been getting even more popular now they could be enjoyed with wonderful views, so we ploughed on for a couple of years – shopping, freezing, cooking, and spending most days in the kitchen from four until nine. We'd been prepared to sacrifice the two thousand pounds a year it made us, but were afraid of losing customers.

It was never going to last. With Debbie working long hours for English Heritage, evening meals were mainly down to me, so I didn't even have a Sybil to sound off to. Whilst I took pride in serving an excellent dinner, the labour involved and the lack of real thanks made it easy to stop. After five years of slaving over a hot stove and cursing brash diners, My Basil took great pleasure in placing the following sign on the Sun Room door:

> *Dinner is no longer served. Go out and find your own. Americans – we recommend the Fat Cafe. Up to the crossroads and follow the stream of saturated fat.*

Ironically, our visitor numbers went up during the following two years, and we attracted guests who took a genuine interest in local pubs and restaurants, feeding us bits of gossip from the ones we recommended, and tipping us off about others we should try or avoid. And it made no difference to our rating – we remained a high quality Four Diamonds Bed and Breakfast.

··· Rare Copper ···

It's not only *how* she spoke, but the looks and silences in between. My Basil wasn't sure whether to humour Felicity Farquhar or try talking the same way.

'It's got potential,' she says, with a dismissive glance round the garden. 'Essay – is thetchor bungalow?'

Everyone asks that question when they walk through the arched rose garden by the giant screen. Perhaps they think it's an annexe with my granny waving. But who was the other lady – in bed by the window? Having her bedroom there exacerbated the privacy issue, especially when mild dementia caused Gladys to make strange gestures which on mute could easily be misconstrued. We were used to it and didn't look across; but guests and visitors were easily drawn.

'No, it's next door,' I reply.

'Extrodnerreh!' Felicity says, crisply. 'Is that alide?'

'It's not ideal,' I say, 'but they're good neighbours.'

'Ay wouldn't be happy with that,' she says. 'You should complain!'

Felicity is from The National Gardens Scheme (NGS) charity, checking whether our garden is suitable for public opening. Having worked on it for five years and visited many others under the Scheme, we *know* it's ready. Densely packed borders, which a visitor might think had been there decades, have replaced large areas of grass, now dedicated to Sunday soccer somewhere – thanks to Jack. Debbie has planted wisely for year-round effect, and I've done the hard landscaping, including reclaiming the bank; visitors can now stroll at brook level close to small shoals of rainbow trout that only abandon their camouflage to dart for a passing insect or dash from someone's shadow.

With few pools deep enough for diving, we've only had one sighting of a kingfisher along our hundred yard stretch, but dippers still nest on a drainage pipe under the road bridge, and we often disturb a feeding heron, the beating wings giving it away before it rises between the trees lining the brook.

The garden stretches away in both directions behind the cottage. At the end away from the giant screen is the orchard from which Bramley apples, Victoria plums and damsons go into crumbles and pies or get given away on the gate. Below this a natural bog garden is kept moist by drainage from the high bank. Plants normally five feet high grow to eight and spread rapidly in the perfect conditions. An old slate mantelpiece set in wild woodruff makes a perfect bench from which to ponder nodding bottle-brush or draw in the sweet scent of giant cowslips.

'Plontsa rother nayce,' says Felicity. 'But you'd heff to meck these steps safe. Insurance, you understand.'

'Yes, of coss,' I say. Debbie prods me in the back.

'End teck extra care by the brook.'

'Yes, of course.'

'End put signs on the road.'

'Yes, of course.'

Posh etiquette makes her tight on compliments, but we *think* picky Felicity approves of the commoners' garden.

Sunday 29th May, 1994 – our first opening. In the NGS directory, alias The Yellow Book, we're listed as "New", always an attraction for garden enthusiasts. Posters are displayed on noticeboards and in shop windows, and press and radio have given us a mention. Earlier in the week we'd recorded an interview with a Radio Shropshire journalist; neither of us had dealt with the media, but our infectious enthusiasm and the sound effects from the waterfall, where the soft shale lining the brook had been cut to a deep chasm over many years, brought the garden to life.

Our road isn't busy, but the nasty bend makes it unsuitable for parking. Half a dozen vehicles will go on our car park; the rest in Geoff's paddock opposite. To organise this, we borrow Chris.

I'd met Chris in The Bridge a year earlier. A short man with a knowing face, he was the only customer one Monday, leaning on the bar contemplating his pint when I walked in. I'd not seen him before; dressed smart casual, with oval spectacles, he looked different from other locals, who were presumably taking an alcohol sabbatical after the rigours of the weekend. Perhaps he was on business, staying in the motel-style accommodation they'd built in the rear car park.

Sometimes a pub has plenty of people, yet nobody talks. Men stand along the bar, a yard apart, happy to share their solitude with like-minded drinkers. Though not engaging with each other, an occasional exchange with the barwoman carries no threat.

'Red sky tonight, Trace.'

'Aar, shepherd's delight. Was red this morning too.'

'Aar, shepherd's warning. Carling please, Trace.'

The irony is that when he leaves, a man will say a warm cheerio to the others as if acknowledging their part in a deep and meaningful discussion they've just had about, say, John Major's views on the Exchange Rate Mechanism. If I said goodbye to all the other passengers as I left a bus or train, and Mrs Thatcher still had any say, I'd be banged up in Shroosbury Gaol.

But with only two people at the bar it can be different. It seems discourteous *not* to talk, embarrassing to stay quiet. It's as if you're the only folk left in the world, marooned at the bar. Not talking would let the other person down – your mate. You're in it together.

It was like that with Chris. We stood at a safe distance, supping Banks's Bitter in silence. There was no background music and Trace was busy elsewhere. It couldn't last and Chris breaks the ice.

'Good bi'urr.'

'Sorry?'

I don't recognise the accent. It's unlike the melodic Norwegian style I'm used to round here.

'Bi'urr's good tonight. Bet'urr 'an where I come frarm.'

'Hm, not bad,' I say, holding up the glass knowingly. 'Where's that then?'

'Brizzle.'

'Sorry?'

'Bristarl.'

'Right. You visiting?'

'No, we're on the new estate.'

In the next three hours Chris and I become chums, setting stools together and swapping pints like reunion friends. He and his wife had moved from a police house in Telford a few months earlier, with Chris on long term sick after an incident at the police station.

'They're finding me a backroom job,' he says, 'or something in the community.'

He already knows a lot about us. At first I put this down to police curiosity – checking out his new patch.

'You got just the two children?' he asks.

'We haven't got any.'

'Oh! Evan said there whirr a family.'

'Yes, we had a family with two teenagers staying last week.'

'Oh.'

'Good choice – Myrrh-cedes 600,' he says after a brief silence, feeling on safer ground. 'Business going well?'

'We haven't got a Mercedes.'

'Oh! Evan said you had a 600 Saloon.'

'We've got an old Golf my dad passed on.'

Even allowing for Evan's creative thinking, it's surprising how people see you as rich working for yourself. It's what our Sussex friends must assume when they don't offer to pay, and locals when they see lots of cars parked outside and an extension being built. Try explaining too hard and you're hiding something. Many of the locals working overtime at the Creamery probably have more cash than us, but if that's what it takes, I'll stick to being a "rich" B&B proprietor.

'He won't be with us long,' says Chris.

'Who – Evan? Why's that? I haven't seen him for a while.'

'Nor me. They say he's got prostate cancer. Has good and bad days.'

'Oh, what a shame! I can never quite work him out, but he's a friendly bloke.'

'Found blood in his water.'

'Oh dear,' I say, lost for words, but glad it wasn't Evan telling me about the blood, because if I hadn't believed him I might have tried making a game of it.

At closing, I offer to walk up with Chris.

'That's okay,' he says. 'I've got the car. Want a lift?'

'You're joking!' I say, assuming he really is. His house is only a few hundred yards away.

'No – you coming?'

'It's okay, I'll walk.'

He toots as he drives past. It's great having a new friend, but somehow the driving spoils it. Not that he's the only one. After eight pints, the guiding principle round here seems to be: 'I'd better make it a half this time – I'm driving.'

I admit to being pious when it comes to drinking and driving, having been on the wrong side of the law in 70s London. Not a good idea screeching round Berkeley Square at one in the morning in a Mini-Moke with six passengers playing air guitar to Led Zeppelin on the radio after being in The Hard Rock Cafe all evening. I got brusque treatment at the police station that night. And for years afterwards, whenever I renewed the car insurance or rented a vehicle, I was greeted with sucked-in breath – clearly not the preserve of estate agents. Since then, *my* guiding principle is to ignore the 'I feel fine, I've only had a couple' driver, and find my own way home.

Funny how you judge someone after three hours and six pints. I felt a frustration in Chris – thwarted in his career, things not working out. I saw a policeman cocking a snook at the law in front of someone he'd never met before. A man moving away from where he'd been a victim, to a fresh community where perhaps he could set his own rules and feel important again.

I knew I liked him, but my gut feeling said: 'Take care.'

'I'll sort the traffic out,' says Chris the day before the opening.

'You sure, Chris? It's a lot of time for you.'

'No problem. I'll bring some signs for the road. "Police Slow".'

While Chris manages the parking in his fluorescent police jacket, Debbie sells plants and I do cream teas from the Sun Room French windows. Coleen comes to look around, even though she and Debbie are in each other's gardens all the time, and John and Meg also support the cause, buying plants we'd normally have given them. Amongst other villagers, Carol (Downy) comes up with her husband and another woman with tiny eyes who looks familiar, and the publicity attracts people from across Shropshire. Debbie, who has struck up a gardening friendship with Carol over recent years, gives them a guided tour while I look after the plants.

The afternoon is a huge success, exhausting but rewarding. Everyone gains. The hundred and fifty visitors love the garden; entry money goes to the NGS; some of the takings go to Minsterley church; and the rest gets put back into the garden. Even Gladys and Violet get a piece of the action as visitors wander past the giant screen.

'Is that your self-catering annexe in the garden?' asks one visitor. 'Two ladies waved at us – one of them in a bed.'

'Yes,' I say. 'It's my great aunties. They're staying a while.'

By the end of the year our fame has spread. The four other openings are well supported; we have our first magazine feature, in *Your Garden*, beautifully written and photographed by a journalist called Trish whom Chris introduced; and a BBC2 team pays a reconnaissance visit with a view to filming the garden for a new series fronted by Stefan Buczacki. Flattering though this is, sadly a helicopter hovers above for much of the visit.

'Do you get many helicopters round here?' asks the Sound Engineer.

'Not really,' I say. 'Only when the police are tracking illegal Albanian immigrants who haven't filled in my Visitors Book properly.'

They never did come to film.

··· 1994 ···

Debbie was lucky to have still been with us for the garden opening.

In March, on her way to work, the Golf was rammed from behind at sixty miles an hour by a large estate loaded with five people and their luggage. Waiting on the crown of the road to turn into Stokesay Castle, where she now worked, the impact forced her across the oncoming lane of the A49. This major North-South route through the Marches usually has back-to-back artics pushing on to their destinations, but at that precise moment there was nothing in sight.

The call from Stokesay frightened me. I was assured Debbie was okay but that her neck hurt and she was in shock. The people in the other car were unscathed. I wanted to be there, but being a one-car household, or by now possibly a nil-car one, I had no way of getting to the scene; until a Jamaican couple from London who'd set up camp in the Tulip Room for three days – heater on, curtains closed in the cold snap – offered to take me. None of us had a mobile phone, so by the time we got to Craven Arms the ambulance had taken Debbie to Shroosbury Hospital in the direction we'd just come from. The kind young couple dropped me off at the hospital where I found Debbie shaken but, according to x-rays, unharmed.

Shortly after the accident, Chris once again proved a true friend. But for his experience, we'd have stayed unaware that Debbie should be eligible for compensation following a whiplash injury. Although she'd had no after-effects from the crash, compensation would be based on the *potential* for neck or back problems later in life.

'See a solicitor,' he said, guiding us through the procedure. 'It's bread-and-butter to them.'

The Telford solicitor gathered information in a matter-of-fact way, including details of Debbie's hospital visit, and a fortnight later we got an offer of five hundred pounds. Excitedly, we told Chris.

'That's rubbish!' he said. 'Turn it down – don't give a reason. You'll get another offer, but you'll probably turn that down too.'

We soon received a letter offering one thousand five hundred which, after consulting our Minsterley legal adviser, we also turned down.

'You'll need to think carefully about the next one,' he said. 'They'll call it a "final" offer and threaten to withdraw altogether if you don't settle.'

As if Chris had been pulling the strings personally, a "final" offer of three thousand pounds duly arrived. Debbie seemed fully recovered, though only time would tell, and we now had the price of a decent holiday.

Later that year, we bought into the new National Lottery, believing it would make us rich beyond belief. How could we *not* win? We stood as much chance as anyone else, and with the prize winner getting about twelve million we'd be set for life. It would take a while before the odds against winning, fourteen million to one, sank in.

But meanwhile we'd won our own lottery – from a man on the A49 who was found, in Ludlow Magistrates Court, to have been driving from Blackpool to South Wales without due care and attention. Our prize – three weeks in Goa, an up-and-coming Indian beach resort sporting the Portuguese heritage we loved. Sumptuous king prawn curries in food shacks along the beach, giant bottles of local Kingfisher lager ("most thrilling chilled" according to the label), and a rich, red ball in the November sky which, like us, local families would watch in awe every evening as it disappeared beyond the sea.

1994 started on a low note but got better and better. We were perfectly primed for our New Year adventure. Starting a family.

⋯ A VIP Arrives ⋯

Late in the pregnancy Debbie elected for a Caesarean. This was a good plan because a) the baby was in breech position, b) the one thing she didn't fancy about having a baby was – *having* the baby, and c) from films I'd seen, an X rating would be insufficient for natural childbirth.

I felt so nervous that I don't recall if it was *Lady in Red* in the background, or some other Chris de Burgh hit. But it was enough to muffle activity behind the curtain and help me distract Debbie with the comforting knowledge that we were saving electricity using the hospital's lighting and that disturbance to B&B guests would be kept to a minimum having the baby in December.

When the nurse placed eight pounds, four and a half ounces of Lily Grace May in my arms I stood mesmerised, tears streaming from my face onto the tiny blanket. For an hour I had Lily to myself. She gripped my little finger tight and I felt the softness of her skin. We shared body warmth and stared at each other, her look saying, 'Don't be scared, dad. I'm here now. We'll be all right.' And I knew we always would be.

That night, in the Beacon pub in Shroosbury, with complete strangers, I wet Lily's head, crying into my Burton's Bitter and de-cluttering myself of layered emotions grown for years like thickening skin. I had the girl I'd hoped for.

'I want a baby,' Debbie had said.

'Hm.'

'I said I'd like to have a baby.'

'Did you? Do you?' I said. 'How about a few beers and a curry instead?'

I'd sailed through to mid-forties without thinking about a family. Alison had never mentioned kids, Debbie didn't fancy childbirth, and so far no-one had turned up with a pram or left a little bundle on the doorstep. Childless friends had encouraged me to think that babies were bad, toddlers were terrible, and civilisation ceased with children of any age. Jim and his wife Angie were especially anti. In a Melbourne restaurant a decade earlier I'd watched them at work.

Three generations of a large Vietnamese family sat round a table spread with their national cuisine. A cosmopolitan buzz filled the room. As the sound of a crying baby filtered through the hum, Angie's ears tilted and rotated towards their table like a dog detecting a noise outside the range of human hearing.

'Do something,' she said, nudging Jim.

Jim put aside his calculator and went into a kind of trance.

'Quiet!' he suddenly shouted, without looking up. Conversation softened, which only made the baby's cry seem louder. No-one looked over.

'Stop that!' he roared from ventriloquist lips.

This time people looked round and the room fell silent – except for the baby, whose wailing now filled the void. Jim hid behind his calculator while Angie smiled across benignly, all of which succeeded in confusing the parents and other diners about where the command had come from.

'They shouldn't bring them here,' said Angie. 'It's not meant for children and we all have to put up with it.'

'And look! They cost a fortune over twenty years!' said Jim, doing a rough calculation and passing me the alarming total on his digital display.

The mother comforted her baby until its sobbing ceased, and a pleasant atmosphere eventually returned. I thought their reaction excessive and embarrassing; but it left me in safe company, not having children of my own.

Then Debbie turned thirty something and the biological clock started ticking. Her vocabulary narrowed down to one word – baby!

'Can't you get one somewhere?' I said, thinking it was a passing fad. Maybe someone at work had brought in a surprisingly well behaved or cheap one.

'I want a baby, and I want it with you.'

'Blimey!' I thought. 'Stealing my name, now my sperm. What's your game?'

We began talking about it seriously and I could see how important it was to Debbie – which made it important to me too.

'It could be years before anything happens,' I thought. But boy, were we fertile! The blue line appeared first hit. And that's when I got it wrong – big time.

'I'm pregnant,' Debbie said, delighted to have fallen so quickly.

'Oh, right,' I said, astonished at the speed things were going, and not immediately grasping the importance of her announcement.

She might have overlooked my 'oh, right', but for the three point five seconds it took me to make it – from the other side of the room. A three

point five seconds credibility gap takes three point five years to close –
minimum. From the other side of the room, double that.

Debbie enjoyed her pregnancy. She asked if I'd come to antenatal
classes but I declined, linking the National Childbirth Trust (NCT) with
middle-class women in long, hessian skirts and insipid men with ponytails
and sandals. Terry nappies and hippy breathing exercises were not for me.
Instead, I got her to drop me off near the venue so I could try some new
pubs and slip in a takeaway before she picked me up later.

When I wasn't smooth-talking guests or buried in an accounts ledger I
shared Debbie's enthusiasm. I was intrigued at the prospect of being a dad,
but in the back of my mind feared that life and livelihood might collapse
like a house of cards.

At ten forty-eight on the morning of Friday 15th December, 1995, that fear
melted away.

··· Bare Pooh ···

I loved life with Lily, but unlike the fathers in Debbie's NCT group, I never
felt like a stereotypical dad in a model family. Perhaps Debbie would have
preferred me that way, but at least I could happily join in their post-natal
get-togethers now that the children were real people and the parties,
though understandably Earth Mother-focussed, had food, alcohol and no
breathing exercises.

Looking after Lily's basic needs – feeding, dressing, nappy-changing –
was as therapeutic and bonding to me as reading to her or playing. I loved
her squeaky giggles and how she suddenly grabbed an object she'd taken a
shine to. And I loved watching her in peaceful sleep.

We took her to the nursery at Pontesbury from about six months, just
a few days a week. Not only did we think this good socially, but it meant
Debbie could return to Stokesay and I could get on with the B&B. After all
it was guests who funded our family life at the cottage.

One aspect of the B &B was not unrelated to nappy-changing.

> **PLEASE NOTE**
> *The cottage has a septic tank, so please flush*
> *nothing more than toilet tissue.*
> *Bin provided below for personal use.*

So says the small sign in each guest bathroom.

We'd been determined to avoid signs around the cottage telling guests not to do this and that. In places we'd stayed ourselves, especially traditional resorts like Torquay and Bournemouth, there were hundreds of them. A bit like National Trust properties – welcoming you, relieving you of your money, but slapping signs everywhere telling you not to touch anything or go beyond the rope cordons behind which they kept the interesting stuff; which, incidentally, left you a narrow channel to shuffle along, tripping over the ankles of people in front and getting barged from behind, all proceeding at the same pace like a chain gang.

'Do you mind!'

'Sorry – the slave behind pushed me into you.'

You're still allowed to look at things though – but I guess that's a matter of time.

The next generation of signs will say:

> *PLEASE*
> *DON'T LOOK AT*
> *ANYTHING*

alongside:

> *NO REFUND FOR*
> *THINGS YOU*
> *HAVEN'T SEEN*

Sometimes, without thinking, I've reached out to touch an intriguing object. I leant towards some armour once in the Clive Museum at Powis Castle. It was like an alarm had gone off in the Jewel House at the Tower of London, only it came from an ancient volunteer in the far corner pretending to read the ancient book resting in her ancient tweed lap.

'Daint touch!' she said, louder than necessary so that everyone else looked round. Perhaps in earlier years she'd barked such commands from the front of an all-girls classroom. I slunk off, wondering if it might have been Felicity Farquar moonlighting.

Give me English Heritage any time. You can clamber to your heart's content over old rocks at Haughmond Abbey or the ruins of Wroxeter Roman City with no fear of upsetting the natives. And at half the price.

As well as conventional notices in B&Bs about emergency evacuation, meal times and private rooms, we'd seen signs like:

Please don't leave hairs in the bath. Others have to use it.

Please leave the toilet as you found it – a silly request if it was already fouled when you got there.

Please remove your shoes at the front door.

Hot water is available between 6 and 9 morning and night.

And that was after we'd worked our way past paintings of distorted animals or non-descript woodland scenes, and holiday photos of fat family members in ill-fitting swimming costumes and silly hats which the owners were certain you'd want to see.

At breakfast, I'd been disappointed not to find:

Take your elbows off the table.

Or:

Sit up straight eating your rubbery fried egg.

So, even though My Basil spends much of his time dreaming up written instructions for guests or roadside notices to discourage ne'er-do-wells, we keep signs to a minimum – septic tank notices, and small plaques saying 'Private' to separate our own quarters. Other information – meal times, restaurant menus, and sketch maps of the cottage and garden – are in a tidy bedroom pack which we show guests when they arrive.

Note to self: practise what you preach about signs; cut down number of notes to self.

Anyone who's never had a septic tank – which we hadn't – may not appreciate the responsibility you take for personal and household waste. Decent drains, a proper tank and a good set of drain rods are standard kit. How to manage the tank, how to clear a blockage and what *not* to put down the toilets is acquired knowledge but just as important.

The idea of a septic tank is that most solids sink in the first chamber and a scum rises to form a 'healthy' crust. Residual liquid works through to a second chamber where remaining solids settle, and the liquid is relatively clear by the time it exits deep into the garden soil via a gravel filter bed which removes final impurities. A properly working tank has little smell and, if cleared every year or so by a waste-removal firm, should last indefinitely.

Ours works fine. The huge two-chambered tank, made of reinforced concrete and capped by three vast concrete slabs, must have been there decades. Modern tanks are usually fibreglass or plastic with an access pipe to the surface, but the less subtle concrete types remain commonplace in rural areas. The clearance man levers open the slabs with an iron bar and brute force, before plunging an industrial vacuum down to suck the contents into a road tanker.

I often recall Jack's tales of waste coming down the valley but I'd seen nothing in the brook to concern me. I suspect he was having us on. I was proud that in our garden at least, we could offer a pure environment to non-paying friends camping only metres away.

Human waste is highly decomposable. But because septic tanks work naturally, introducing foreign objects or using too many toilet chemicals interferes with the process. In a landfill site tampons and cotton buds take up to a year to decompose, condoms (like rubber tyres) are estimated at fifty years, and disposable nappies or sanitary towels five to eight hundred. In a septic tank these items will not only fail to break down, but will inhibit the tank's ability to deal with the human stuff, leading to unwarranted smells and costly extra clearance.

We can control what chemicals we use in the cottage and what we put down our own toilet, but not what guests decide in the privacy of their own rooms. And when someone who can't read or doesn't care flushes something they shouldn't, it may not even reach its target. There are many bends to negotiate twixt loo and tank; as with road traffic, if one person gets it wrong a pile-up can occur. And clearing up after a bad crash is no-one's idea of fun – whether on the road *or* under a manhole cover in my back garden path. Rodding a blocked drain – possibly the least glamorous occupation in the world.

⋯   Out and About   ⋯

I'd worried I might not get out so much after Lily was born. Debbie had always shared my liking for trips to gardens or tea shops and going for a drink once or twice a week. But she was more settled than me. Where Debbie was happy following Bergerac or Casualty on TV or doing something creative at home, I'd be itching to see what was going on elsewhere. So I continued going out several nights a week, and though she occasionally joined me with Lily, Debbie seemed content at home, especially if she'd been at work during the day. Or that's how I chose to see it.

The Horseshoes at Pontesbury was now my local. As fellow devotees of real ale, both Chris and Bill the Vicar, as we'd come to know our local clergyman, had found the pub to their taste, even though it's further away than the two remaining Minsterley pubs. (The Bath Arms, which had always been the weakest link in the BBC, had been replaced by housing, showing that even the Creamery's presence couldn't keep three pubs going). Jim and Barbara run a good pub; Jim's knowledge of sport and world events makes great listening, and Barbara does a fine scampi and chips, so I was easily won over. The only down side was having to drive. Debbie was usually happy to do so, but if I was going alone I'd try to make it a Friday or Saturday, when she would drop me off and I could flag down the late bus home.

I discovered a handy Tuesday bus. Plox Green is halfway between Shroosbury and Bishops Castle, and believe it or not there was a timetabled bus to Bishops Castle on a Tuesday evening, ostensibly to take teenage lads to Cadet Corps. Perversely, I could get across the hills by public transport to sleepy BC, but not along the main road to Shroosbury in the other direction. This was too good to waste, and I took to catching the Cadet bus every few weeks.

'Thought I'd pop into Bishops Castle,' I'd say, with increasing regularity. 'You don't mind, do you?'

'Do you have to?' Debbie would say.

'Well not if you don't want me to.'

'No. You go, if that's what you want.'

'Be back by ten,' I'd say.

At 6.30 I'd stand at Plox Green crossroads in the freezing dark, listening for the familiar diesel chug of the vintage 30-seater heading up from Minsterley. As its lights approached I'd jump into the road waving like the Railway Children to make sure they saw me. Propped high in the driver's seat would be a middle-aged woman with an ill-fitting cardigan, like she'd popped out during dinner to do the run.

'I'll do your pudding when I get back, John.'

The service was operated by M&J Travel, a family business from Newcastle – not the Northumberland or Stoke one, but a remote hamlet near Craven Arms. The woman would drive the half hour from there to Minsterley, run the twenty-five minutes back to Bishops Castle, return to Newcastle for pudding, and reverse the trip later in the evening. It cost me a quid or something silly. The ancient, rattling bus might stop to pick up a couple of cadets at the Bentlawnt turn in Hope Valley or at Lydham, but more often than not I'd have a personal taxi service each way if parents had taken over transport duty.

No Bishops Castle pub went untried, but I'd usually settle for the wonderful panelled bar in the Castle Hotel with its hollowed leather chairs and a roaring coal fire. The scatty woman of the house would stoke the fire and work the kitchen, while the man lorded it up with locals. If I didn't find a fellow drinker I'd set the world right by myself.

After three or four pints of Hobsons Bitter there'd still be time for a quick chicken saag at the nearby Ganges BYO (Bring Your Own), washed down with a bottle of Hobsons Pale Ale from the pub – no late night Co-op in those days. Then I'd shiver down the hill under a starry sky to wait at a pre-arranged place for the freezing 9.30 return trip. The heady days of subsidised buses.

Lily did not want for getting out and about. We'd introduced her to the Horseshoes while still in her carry chair, and being new grandparents themselves, Jim and Barbara took a real interest in watching her grow up. Around her first birthday Lily got into foreign travel, as we spent four winter weeks at Nerja in the South of Spain, the first two unbroken sunshine, the last two unbroken rain with mould spreading across the apartment ceiling and mushrooms growing on the inside of the front door. Debbie's mum ('Nanny') joined us just in time for the rainy bit. For a one year old, Lily was an impeccable traveller – not a peep on the plane in spite of our concern about changes in air pressure, and still small enough to go everywhere in a back carrier.

'I'll keep an eye on the cottage for you,' Chris had said.

It was the first time we'd been away that long and it seemed unfair asking a neighbour. John and Meg were often away themselves, and Geoff and Colleen were always busy. Had it been the early years, Jack would have relished the task; in the six months before we moved into Cricklewood Cottage he'd kept a watchful eye between our weekend visits. But to ask Violet, for whom Jack had done everything, would have been wrong.

'I miss 'im dreadful,' she'd remind us most weeks, before closing the door on herself. It had been six years now, and although family visited, it was hard to imagine a more desolate person. The once inquisitive face peering out from the giant screen had been replaced by a shrunken figure kneeling for hours on a damp living room floor. She wouldn't let anyone carry out remedial work; if Jack couldn't do it, then nobody else would. When Gladys had had to move to the Minsterley Care Home earlier in the year, it seemed to take away the last part of Violet's purpose in life.

We gratefully accepted Chris's offer. The cats were in a cattery, but security was an issue since there was open access to the garden and the rear of the building. With his "local policeman" hat on, Chris was the obvious man, and revelled in the task. By now he was established in a community role, successfully developing the Safe-Hands Scheme through schools and shops, its clasped-hands logo in the windows of most Shroosbury stores. Lost children were encouraged to recognise this sign, knowing they'd be safely looked after in that shop until reunited with a parent.

It was wonderful being away a whole month – reward for our hard work and one of the benefits of being self-employed. Chris was a thorough minder and we valued his friendship more than ever. The only downside was that, in spite of his running the engine of our latest Golf several times, the damp weather left a coat of black mould across the white vinyl interior. Back from Spanish mould to a home-grown variety.

The irony was that the day before we left, a caller from Toronto, enquiring about summer accommodation, had raised this very subject.

'Tell me, do you have any mould?' he'd said. The likeness to an American accent, even though I could recognise the difference and knew that Canadians shunned Americans, put me on the defensive.

'Yes, my house is full of it. Is there any particular type you were looking for? I have Shropshire mould – and I could look for some Andalucian while I'm away; I hear it's pretty good stuff.'

'My wife has an allergy to it,' he said, 'so we always ask beforehand.'

It reminded me of Fothergill being asked if his beds were well-aired. This was his way of dealing with it:

'Well, I would imagine the dampness or dryness of the beds is that of the surrounding atmosphere, and even if you do shut the windows on damp days, sooner or later the beds would become damp in spite of your efforts . . . and I would submit that after a bed has been slept in it is wetter than it was before by the amount of moisture the sleeper has exuded from his person during the night.'

If the Canadian man had phoned on our return, I'd have had more of the subject to talk about, but my reassurance was enough for the couple to come and stay the following year. I'd always been vigilant about removing signs of bathroom mould, since its presence was a prime example of where **not** to stay. But for Mr and Mrs Black I made a note in the diary to fetch out the Mould and Mildew Remover the day before they arrived, just in case.

The following spring we spent a chilly week in a caravan at Fallbarrow Park on the banks of Lake Windermere. Going away in April was a rare treat. Bowness was a safe family town, the greatest danger coming from the over-friendly lakeside swans which were of dinosaur proportion to Lily in her push chair. The Beatrix Potter exhibition, where life-size Peter Rabbit and Benjamin Bunny reminded Lily of our real pets back home, was inspirational, as was a trip to Beatrix Potter's home at Hill Top Farm in the tiny village of Near Sawrey, where Lily could look for Jemimah Puddleduck's eggs hidden in the garden.

'There! There!' she'd say, pointing excitedly with a curled forefinger, just finding her voice.

Closer to home, we'd stroll around Snailbeach, exploring the fascinating industrial ruins from lead-mining days – pit shafts, railway tracks, the blacksmith's shop, a double-walled gunpowder arsenal and grand Cornish engine houses, all preserved for posterity in the wooded hillside.
'There! There!'

When Lily was two, and rushing around, we spent Christmas in Madeira, a winter retreat we'd re-visited twice since our honeymoon, guaranteed mild if not sunny, and very much Portuguese. Although treks along levadas, Madeira's fascinating, man-made irrigation channels cut into the mountain sides to bring water from the central rainy areas down to the cultivated Southern regions, were not practical this time, we got out and about in Funchal's parks and on the floating waterfront cafes, where Lily could throw crumbs to the mullet and gaze in awe at the huge cruise ships that dominated the deep harbour. Having themselves taken a shine to the island, my parents joined us that year for a memorable family Christmas.

And we followed Madeira with a fortnight in sunny Lanzarote, also a volcanic island but with the added drama of black rock formations, and with safe, sandy beaches for Lily to rush around on.

My surprise Algarve holiday back in 1991 had set the tone for our winter escapes. With little B&B money spare for holidays, Debbie's work paid for most trips, and with prices at their lowest and warm winter weather only four hours away, it had become a great way to end a busy year. All the better for Lily coming with us.

··· At Home ···

Once she was on her feet, Lily could enjoy the garden as much as we did. We'd watch her turn up a flower head and sniff inside, and she'd point at aeroplanes – 'There! There!' – or chase birds down the path with a squeal of excitement, turning to distress when she fell over. Debbie's rabbits, Joshua,

Thumper and Dillon, weren't much smaller than Lily. Each of their large hutches had a run of rough grass, and Lily would feed them clumps of fresh dandelion leaves with a look of great concentration.

The cottage was at the centre of an elliptical plot. At the back the brook could rise from three inches to three feet in a matter of hours if torrential rain consumed the valley. When it was three inches and crystal clear you *shared* life with the brook – collecting stone, cutting back branches, marvelling at this miracle running alongside the garden; but at three feet, chocolate brown and surging like a tsunami, you allowed it sole rights. And to the front of the cottage the little traffic that used the road did so at a fair old lick.

I built a secure fenced area for Lily behind the cottage in a patch containing the hutches, and she was rarely left alone. But people still worried.

'What about the brook?' they'd say.

'What about it?' we'd say.

'Lily might drown,' they'd say.

'She might love watching the trout,' we'd say.

'What about the road?'

'What about it?'

'She might get run over.'

'Only if we let her.'

This aspect of parenting falls roughly into two styles. The first cocoons children to minimise the chance of an accident; those parents would have quit Cricklewood Cottage before having their baby. The second, which included Debbie and me, keeps an eye out but lets them experience as much as possible. In the same way that nursery from an early age was to show Lily how to play and share, we wanted her to understand real life, and her imaginative commentary on what she discovered rewarded us many times over.

We both enjoyed reading to Lily, especially at bedtime; when it was my turn it was wonderful watching her eyes grow wide as the story came to life. She loved being read to. Once she'd heard a story two or three times and knew the plot she'd break in and say what was going to happen next. Lily was always confident, and it was good being able to communicate with a two year old in a relatively grown-up way yet still indulge my childlike side.

Debbie's work pattern meant it often fell to me to collect Lily from the nursery. I'd proudly watch her from a distance before she spotted me and rushed over to be picked up or to show me a work of art she'd created earlier. Back at the cottage we'd play or read or see what we could find in the garden or on TV, until Debbie returned to start a fresh round of nurturing. I savoured my private moments with Lily, each one reinforcing our father-daughter relationship.

One of my favourite morning tricks was to tap on the outside of her bedroom window (Ron's old room at the back), like blackbirds tap for currants. After a while I'd see the curtains twitch and her innocent smile appear between the join as she rocked the cot excitedly. Sometimes I'd huff on the window and plant a kiss mark, making her giggle, and she'd try one back without really knowing how. Welcome to another day, Lily.

··· Love Nest ···

Cricklewood Cottage is perfect for a romantic weekend break. The room names – Rose, Bow and Tulip – have an enchanting feel, with their polished oak beams and gorgeous views over the hills. As word spreads, many couples come to stay more than once.

A young man with a sports saloon travelled from London four times in consecutive months, asking for the Bow Room each time. We never saw much of him or his lady friend; just enough to notice it was a different woman each time – and offer a diplomatic smile.

Another time I received a lunchtime call from a man wanting a double room. Pushing aside my helpful information about room and price, his only concern was did it have a double bed and was it free now. It was a quiet time of year, and with all three rooms unoccupied his trade was welcome. Arriving at three o'clock, the couple retired directly to the Bow Room and, apart from one brief absence for pizza, didn't emerge for forty-eight hours. Apparently the man was a builder from across the hills in Church Stretton and had a reputation for "finding" women and whisking them off at short notice – although how Geoff knew that I really don't know. The cottage resounded to their special brand of entertainment, and I was honoured to have been part of his exciting lifestyle.

John Fothergill would have had none of this. One of his pet hates was 'indiscriminating couples'. No love nest, The Spreadeagle. His trade was built on fine dining and hosting the 'right kind of undergrad and better class don from Oxford', or those of a similar class in what he called the 'outer world'. A lesser person was likely to have 'invaded that fortress of Victorian gentility, of the serviette, sugar tongs, fish knives, not passing on stairs, hat lifting and not licking your fingers . . .'

And he painted a wonderful picture of Oxford youth:

'The occasional Oxford lad who brings a shop girl disturbs me . . . we have the respect of all the best undergraduates . . . these shop girls must not come and spoil the show.'

And:

'The dinner was spoilt for me by two undergraduates . . . bringing two girls, almost certainly Oxford hacks.'

Though always making his opinion clear, he sometimes softened his tone:

'Two young men with two handsome women of the bright young high-brow type asked for double beds. In the morning I said to the young men: 'last night, of course, the fog threw you at us, but we are not good here at mixed couples.''

On other occasions, he couldn't be bothered:

'Four people took four single rooms, only two of which they quickly monopolized with a deal of mixed bathing. I never looked at them again for the rest of their two-day stay, for once too bored to argue my convictions.'

Perhaps the most starry-eyed lovebirds were two guys about my age from Australia. On arrival they stood in the Reading Room, and without having seen any of the cottage or garden became quite gushing.

'The colours in the garden – they're simply *magnificent*,' said the balding one.

'And the decorations,' said his friend, 'you've got them *just* right.'

I played along for a while, always keen to be flattered. Mindful that it was introductory small talk, I tried moving the conversation on, but the effusive Ozzies were having none of it.

'The rooms are *so* tasteful . . .'

After ten minutes it had become tiresome. Of greater concern was how both men were staring at me, adoringly. One of them was foaming at the lips, a thin dribble running down the side of his chin, and both were sweating profusely. Debbie and Lily were in Sussex that week, and no matter how irrational it might seem, I felt uneasy on my own. Fortunately the phone rang and I was able to leave them waxing lyrical until I came back to show them to their room – by which time they'd calmed down a bit.

I took guilty pleasure teasing a young man on the phone about, ahem, things not to leave behind.

'Hello, we stayed with you at the weekend and I think I might have forgotten my spectacles,' he says, nervously.

'Right. I don't remember seeing any, but I'll have a look. Which room was it?'

'The one with its own staircase. They might be under the bed.'

'The Rose Room. Just a minute – I'll have a look.'

Sure enough, I find his glasses in a soft case pushed a foot under the double bed. Alongside are some condoms, one foil-sealed, the other less pristine. I give him the news – about the specs, at least.

'Oh, that's good,' says the young man. 'Er, was there anything else with them?'

I'm not sure why he asks, since his private life is not my business and there's no inherent value in the condoms, especially one of them. Lying is the easiest ploy.

'No – there was nothing else,' (and quickly moving on), 'would you like me to send the glasses?'

'Yes please,' he says. 'Er, I think it might be best if you use my work address, and can you please mark them as private, for my personal attention.'

'Sure,' I say, 'what's the address?'

Chuckling to myself, I post the evidence to Mr Worried of a library somewhere in Lancashire, clearly a hotspot for extramarital shenanigans. They were a nice couple, who sadly never came back.

··· Going It Alone ···

A love nest for visitors Cricklewood Cottage may well be. But as 1998 wears on, I sense that my own future with Debbie is not so bright. We've achieved a lot in our ten years at Cricklewood Cottage and in Brighton before that. The business is sound and a respected part of the community, the garden has matured delightfully, Lily has graced our lives and we've made good friends.

But when people see different ways forward and can't reconcile them, the drive to move on gets overpowering. Whilst Debbie and I equally embrace Lily as part of our lives, I do so against a backdrop of the B&B and freedom to push on socially, whilst Debbie searches for a more settled family home and greater privacy.

Things have been awkward for some time, and I suspect that before long I'll be running the cottage alone. No bitterness or recrimination; just one of those things – time for the next phase.

'We need to talk,' I said, as Debbie was about to leave for work, having dropped Lily off at the nursery. The tension had got too much for me and I needed answers. I'd rehearsed that opening line a hundred times, but it still came out like some awful movie cliché.

'This evening,' she said. 'I'm late already.'

'No – now. You'll have to be late.'

Any other day she'd have asserted herself, but something in my tone alerted her to the urgency. We'd always been good at talking things through, and it became clear, as I thought, that Debbie had made her mind up. She wanted a life with choices of her own, not always bound by the needs of Cricklewood Cottage. I was still letting the business rule the household and trying to pursue an active social life of my own at a time when family should have taken preference. And it didn't help that My Basil had been showing his hand more than ever. We were simply growing apart.

I wasn't worried at the thought of being alone. I'd always had an independent streak and privately accepted that the change could be positive. My concern was Lily. She was two and a half and we'd formed a strong bond; whilst I knew she needed to be with her mother, I was floundering at the prospect of not seeing her so often.

I'd pre-ordered a birthday cake for Debbie which would have been churlish to cancel. The so-called reputable cake-maker in Shroosbury must have had a premonition because the characters topping the cake came out like distorted creatures from a bargain-basement horror movie, and the one that was supposed to be Debbie had oversize, horn-rimmed glasses like the ugly girl in class. Handing her the cake was like saying, 'This is how I see you!'

And as if in sympathy, Oliver the cat, who'd been with us since Brighton days and had lost his mate Thomas to a fast car the previous year, decides to call it a day too. Eighteen and ailing, he has to be put down.

11th August 1998. I wasn't there when Debbie and Lily went away. We thought it best for Lily that they leave before I returned from a break in Cornwall. Phone chats with Lily from a call box in Looe had been hard, but she sounded fine and that's what mattered.

Just three weeks since it all came out. It's strange walking back into an empty cottage – no guests or family. The evening sun highlights the warm walls round the inglenook, shadows changing by the minute. As I open a bottle of whisky I feel a strong sense of "starting again". I'll miss Lily – her room seems eerily quiet. But they're renting a house up the road and I'll be staying at the cottage. Everything will be all right – I think.

···   On Yer Bikes   ···

It was many years since Debbie had been properly involved in the B&B, but she'd kept it ticking over if I was catching up in Brighton or taking a recovery break in Llandudno. The occasional blips – serving a teapot of boiling water with no teabags or presenting one table with a pot of cold tea just cleared from another – could be put down to rustiness, and were a source of amusement not complaint.

There's a routine to breakfasts and cleaning rooms. With a maximum of six guests, usually fewer, I'd always managed by myself with plenty of time for shopping, gardening and a snooze. But now officially a one-man band, I put in extra measures – staggering breakfast times and getting new visitors to say when they expected to arrive. As ever, most guests are keen to help and the system works well. I even arranged for one couple (who'd stayed before, so knew their way around) to collect the keys from me on their way past the Horseshoes. Now that's what I call good management! Many are curious about my domestic arrangements though.

'Is your wife away at the moment?'

'Well there *is* only me,' I reply, which usually does the trick.

A couple doing a John O'Groats to Land's End tandem ride, one of many cycling parties who'd chosen the scenic route and offered welcome business, clearly have no idea why I'm there.

'Do you work?' says the man.

'If I didn't, sir, you wouldn't be getting any breakfast!'

'This *is* my work,' I say.

A medium-fat American woman asks, 'Are you retired?'

'Well, madam, if the only alternative you understand is being slave to a huge American corporation, working sixteen hours a day for a pittance, under constant threat of being fired for not meeting unreasonably high targets, then yes, call me retired.'

'No, this is my job,' I say, dizzy from counting the spots on her leopard-skin jacket.

A thoughtful guest from Norwich praises the effort that has gone into the 'marvellous rooms and pretty garden'.

'How do you manage with just the two of you?'

I look around, expecting a second person to have crept up on me like in a pantomime.

'Well there *is* only me.'

Even on the busiest weekends, I'm okay. By far the biggest event locally is the Shroosbury Flower Show. One of Britain's biggest summer flower shows, it attracts up to sixty thousand people over a Friday and Saturday in mid-August. The twenty-nine acre Quarry Park, with the Dingle its colourful centrepiece, is taken over by giant marquees and trade stands, celebrity chefs and horticulturalists giving talks and demonstrations, and exhibitors enjoying their busiest weekend of the year. With the Quarry on a steep slope down to the River Severn, the Shropshire Horticultural Society prays for fine weather on Show weekend. Persistent rain makes it impossible to get around; in 1970, play was halted on the first day after two inches of rain fell in as many hours.

Percy Thrower, MBE, father of gardening on television and radio and Shropshire's main claim to horticultural fame, was much involved with the Society. Both his father and father-in law had been head gardeners, the latter at the Royal Gardens of Sandringham and Windsor Castle where Percy had started work as a journeyman gardener. In 1946 he became Superintendent of Parks at Shroosbury, staying until his retirement in1974, and the Percy Thrower Garden Centre he opened to the south of Shroosbury stayed under his daughters' control after he died in 1988.

For major events like the Flower Show, B&Bs in Shropshire fill up quickly. By Easter most rooms are taken. The Tourist Information Centre phones round before the Show to find last minute vacancies, but these are few. Late bookers or tourists unwittingly arriving in the area might have to stay as far afield as Ludlow or Oswestry, twenty-five miles away.

We had soon realised it made sense to specify a minimum period of stay on these weekends – in our case two nights. With demand high there was little point in the added chore of daily room changes, but in reality most guests stayed three or four nights and visited other attractions, especially if they'd not stayed in the area before. If we'd said yes to everyone who enquired we'd have needed a fifty-bedroom hotel – maybe that's what Evan Davies had envisaged. It was as frustrating for us turning customers away as it must have been for them, but we soon learnt that viewing it as lost business was a false premise, and valued the guaranteed custom we *did* get.

At peak times people who didn't normally offer B&B tried to help with overspill. John and Meg opened their doors on one occasion, and Colleen was always willing to help out. Aside from event weekends she'd take guests from us overnight when we might otherwise lose, say, a six day booking because we were full on just one of those days. This worked well and we both gained. It had all started on the one occasion I double-booked a room.

'Hello,' says the travel-weary man at my doorstep. 'Mr Woodward. We have a room booked.'

'Have you?' I say, knowing all three rooms are already taken. 'Are you sure you've got the right place? This is Cricklewood Cottage,' I add, pointing towards the house sign.

'Yes, I know it's Cricklewood Cottage,' he says. 'That's why we're here. We have a room booked. We've just driven from Kent.'

'I'm sorry, my guests have already arrived,' I say, as if that proves he's wrong.

'Well, would you check your diary, please,' he says. 'I'll let my wife know there's a problem.'

While he's back in the car park, I discover they've booked for five nights starting the following day, which is why I hadn't been expecting them. I never found out how this happened, but clearly I have to make other arrangements. I try other B&Bs to no avail, but fortunately Colleen comes to the rescue. The Woodwards are gracious enough to accept there's been a misunderstanding, and stay with her on their first night.

'They seemed to like it. I hope so, anyway,' said Colleen next day. 'We quite enjoyed having someone in, now we're not working so much.'

Geoff had sold his share of the farm to his brother, and he and Colleen had bought a flat on the Costa del Sol. Though retired from her job at the Creamery, Colleen still helped there at busy times, as did Geoff at the farm, but now they could spend more time tending their beautiful brookside garden and getting away to Spain several times a year.

And the Woodwards' stay had opened up another way of life – taking guests on an occasional basis. Other than Christmas, they often helped us out on public holiday weekends, which could be as busy as the Flower Show. Christmas enquiries were few; for the first two years we were open as normal, but people wanted a festive package which we didn't offer. It soon became clear that November to February would be our quietest time, enabling us to get away without losing "money in", so I'd acceded to Debbie's suggestion that we officially closed for several days over the Christmas period.

There were other events that proved quieter for B&B than we'd been led to believe. The Minsterley Show and the Shropshire Steam Engine Rally were important to the community economically and socially, and the Minsterley Eisteddfod brought in huge crowds over a March weekend.

Neighbours would tell us, 'You'll be busy this weekend, then?' But unlike the Flower Show, these events attracted people on a day trip only, and gave us no extra business.

For the Eisteddfod, choirs were bussed in and out daily from Wales and the West Midlands to do their turn at the vast Minsterley Parish Hall. Fringe events, in the form of ad hoc performances by wonderful Welsh male voice singers, were held in the lounge bar at the Bridge. Free choir with every pint of Banks's – a bargain!

The Eisteddfod had been Evan's favourite occasion, and since he passed away in 1995 a song had been sung for him in the pub each year.

'Do you sing?' I'd asked him at one of the pub gigs.

'Aar, should do where I come from,' he said. 'Couldna reach them high notes though.'

'Don't know how they do it,' I said.

'Daresay they've got their trousers done up tight,' he said, with a mischievous grin.

'You'd know all about doing trousers up,' I thought.

Instead of his usual sleeveless number, Evan would dress up specially. A tee shirt with a Welsh dragon, his baggy trousers pulled up over the dragon's tail. I'll swear I saw a tear trickle down his cheek as men from the valleys sang their sad way through each beer placed as currency on the table beside them.

'Sang on the cruise ships for years,' said Evan. 'Went all over the world. Mediterranean, Caribbean – Antarctic.'

'Sing with the penguins, did you?'

'Aar,' he said with conviction, before a cheeky grin from the old feller doubled us both up with laughter.

How lucky, I thought, to have such exquisite singing brought to my doorstep every March, uniting the village like Christmas. And to have seen Evan getting so much pleasure from it.

A major local event that did offer good business was the annual mountain bike racing at Eastridge Woods, a Forestry Commission site a mile or so from Minsterley in the lower reaches of the Stiperstones. Part of the British Mountain Bike Series, the event fetches hundreds of people into the area – young contestants, their families and supporting entourage. But whereas the Flower Show attracted our kind of customer in personality and horticultural passion, the bike event did pretty much the opposite.

There was nothing inherently wrong with younger people staying, but as with Creamery contractors, the character of the cottage was lost on them. The predictable traits of teen lads – untidiness, complete disregard

for the wellbeing of someone's home, and the ability to eat you out of it –
were one thing, but they also had an obsessive compulsion about fitness
and all things bike.

Take the bikes. Okay – they were usually top of the range machines
worth a bob or two, and needed looking after. But my padlocked shed wasn't
good enough for them, and I had a fight to stop bikes being surreptitiously
brought into the cottage and dumped against the Colefax and Fowler. It got
like shooing out a stray cat that had found its way through the cat flap but
kept slinking back in when you weren't looking.

One day in the Tulip Room, being shared by two lads, I found a bike
upside down on its handlebars, half dismantled. The front wheel was
leaning against the antique fireplace, the chain was in the sink, and various
spanners and oil cans were scattered around. With no sign of a protective
sheet, my carpet was taking the full brunt. Realistically, if I'd suggested one
the tykes would probably have used the crocheted bedspread.

'Out you go! Shoo!'

And take the fitness. To keep themselves in tip-top racing condition, these
lads have a strict eating regime, with carbohydrates the main component.
Until we stopped offering evening meals they fuelled themselves every
night with pasta and potatoes, and at breakfast, porridge, cereals and toast
were top of the list.

I'm closely interrogated as to what I can offer. None of it is a problem for
My Basil, but the way it's demanded is.

'Haven't you got any brown rice?' says Lee, a particularly stroppy
adolescent.

'Only **baked** beans?' says his mate, Marvin. 'I need pinto beans to
maximise my energy level.'

'I didn't realise teenagers had an energy level,' says My Basil. *'By the
way, I just went and scratched your bike.'*

'I'll see what I can find,' I say.

'I'd like my porridge and yoghurt at 8.43, an hour and seven minutes
before my first race, to yield maximum energy per unit of oxygen I consume,'
says Lee.

*'Will you be up by then? I thought all teenagers stayed in bed till
lunchtime.'*

'I'll see what I can do.'

I feel used and abused. But that's not the end of it; the Reading Room
has turned into a harem. While one lanky lad has his legs over the arm of
a chair, presumably at the prescribed angle for perfect blood circulation,
the other chair is being used as a massage couch. Leighton lounges in

underpants while his girlfriend Jackie (his support team) lubricates his thighs with what smells like Ambre Solaire. Little grunts trip from his lips with each upward thrust, and his legs jig uncontrollably. I daren't look too closely but he seems really happy. It's a lot for a forty-seven year old to have to deal with in his own home.

'*Take your hands off that boy! This is not a brothel.*'

'Would you please do that in your room?' I say, when things seem to be going too far.

Here's the rub. Like any other customers, I value Jackie and Leighton's patronage, and I *have* invited them into my house. But if I treat customers with respect it should be reciprocal, and these young people wouldn't recognise reciprocal if it smacked them in the head. It's a measure of their adolescence that if I ask nicely they ignore me, but when I take a fatherly hand, evicting bikes from the bedroom workshop, they accept it without question. Just like I accepted at twenty-three being thrown out by the landlady of a shared house in Fulham for using the bath to work on my mini engine; sadly my three housemates had to go too.

I wonder what Fothergill would have made of it. In 1926 he'd noted similar problems:

'I had to talk to an undergraduate for sprawling about on his chair and putting his feet on the mantel-shelf.'

And:

'A semi-drunk Oxford tradesman is to report me to the RAC for my telling him not to sit on one of his two tart's knees in the Common Room.'

Dreadful!

After more than a decade, the mountain bikers find a deserved place on the "cutting it out" list. Their business has been reliable and good, but after one year dealing with them on my own I decide the aggravation outweighs the benefit.

In the Autumn of 1999, Leighton, sixteen, sprawled on the cream, mock-leather, DFS sofa at his home in Hemel Hempstead, spots the following small ad in Mountain Biking UK magazine:

> *I am not a workshop, a massage parlour or a branch of Holland and Barrett. So get on yer bikes, and take your obsession elsewhere. My Basil.*

··· Moving On ···

Nothing that happened between me and Debbie got in the way of our love for Lily. Other than a short initial period when they stayed in Sussex with Debbie's mum, and we'd meet halfway in tranquil parkland, they lived within ten miles of Cricklewood Cottage, quickly settling into a delightful, Victorian semi at Lydham – called Lily Cottage! With its original green-enamelled name plate and a wonderful mature garden, it was ideal for Lily to grow up in, and only fifteen minutes away. I still collected her from nursery, and she'd stay with me every week or so in her newly decorated bedroom, now with a child's bed instead of a cot. We were lucky.

A year to the day after they left, the three of us sat in the back garden at Cricklewood Cottage awaiting a rare event. A total eclipse of the sun was due on 11th August 1999 at about eleven in the morning. It was good sharing this. A lot had happened during the year, some of it uncomfortable to deal with, and being together for such a memorable occasion was part of the healing process.

We explained as best you can to a three and a half year old how a total solar eclipse occurs when the dark silhouette of the moon completely obscures the bright light of the sun, and for a minute or so leaves a brilliant corona round its edge. Like the last major natural phenomenon in Plox Green, the earthquake of 1990, it had been the talk of the village, only this time beforehand and not in the aftermath.

Following copious advice not to look directly at the sun, we sat waiting with special cards ready to cover our eyes. It turned out to be a damp squib; the cloud cover showed no sign of shifting and you even had to guess where the sun was. But we were awestruck in an unexpected way. Around the scheduled time, it came over gloomy like dusk, with an eerie silence setting in. We realised that the hundreds of noisy birds normally circling above and flitting between hedgerows had stopped singing and returned to roost. Instinctively, we too fell silent, hearing only the trickling brook below. As lovers of the countryside, that would prove as strong a memory as any eclipse.

We'd always taken Lily on day trips, the seaside most popular. Aberystwyth was the nearest, and the two hour drive through dramatic Welsh hill country full of anticipation. The old-fashioned seaside resort of Borth and fine dunes of Ynyslas at the mouth of the River Dovey were great places for Lily to discover the sea and meet other children, making sandcastles or digging a hole so deep that bobbing sunhats were the only sign of life.

Lily and I adopted Aberdovey as our special retreat, on the opposite side of the river from Ynyslas whose dunes you could see shimmering in the sun. We'd splash about cautiously in the fast river current and collect shells from the soft sand higher up the beach, stepping round mounds of bubbly seaweed and huge slabs of dead jellyfish.

Crabbing on the pier was compulsory. Using strips of mackerel as bait, there'd be intense competition with other holidaymakers to catch the most crabs for our brightly coloured buckets of sea water, and afterwards a race to see whose would get back to the sea first. As soon as you released them on the beach they'd start their unfaltering sideways charge; we never did understand how they knew which way to go.

We began staying overnight. The landlady at the B&B above the Post Office took a shine to Lily, and we visited several times before they sold up. At the age of four, Lily would stomp up the stairs with her child's suitcase as if it was her second home.

'Have you brought Grandad with you?' said Jenny on one visit, as Lily slogged up behind her.

'Dad, actually,' I said, laughing to relieve Jenny's embarrassment.

Lily loved her seaside stays. We'd fill the car with important paraphernalia – buckets and spades, rubber rings, beach games – and off we'd go. She'd make friends easily in playgrounds and on the beach, wanting to swing higher than the others and clamber upside down on rope mazes in an alarming way. On duller days we'd take a train to Barmouth along the coastal line cut into the cliff face a hundred feet above Cardigan Bay and over the iconic timber bridge across the Mawddach estuary. And at Twyn she used the promenade to practise bike riding, or we might take the narrow gauge Talyllyn Railway up through beautiful scenery to the old slate mining areas, stopping for tea at the Quarryman's Tea Room while we waited for the return train.

The strong bond between Lily and me was something to treasure. I was to stay at Cricklewood Cottage for the foreseeable future, leaving her a stable base and creating income for all of us. By the time she started at Bishops Castle Primary School Lily was a confident girl, proud as a peacock in her blue school uniform.

As well as seeing each other outside the B&B, I liked her sharing my work life. Sometimes she chose a role of her own. When new guests arrived, curiosity would get the better of her, and if I wasn't quick enough she'd take over.

'Breakfast is in the Sun Room,' she'd say, familiar with my daily mantra. 'My room's through there.'

'And how old are *you*?' a grandmother type would ask.

'I'm four and three quarters,' Lily would say, resolute about the three quarters but itching to justify, 'I'm nearly five.'

Her chosen task at breakfast was taking the toast.

'Shall I take the toast, or do you want to?' I call out, as she watches TV in the lounge.

'I will, I will!' she says, abandoning ***Bear in the Big Blue House*** and trotting to the kitchen in a panic.

She steps gingerly towards the Sun Room, carrying the racked toast on a plate, staring intently as if delivering rare gifts.

'Hello dear,' I hear. 'Thank you – that's lovely. And what are *you* doing today?'

'Erm, I'm going to Sainsbury's with my dad, then I might do some cycling in the playground at Minsterley School. I'm allowed to when it's closed, you know, because Jack and Abigail go there.'

'Oh, that's nice,' grandmother-person says. 'Have a lovely time, dear.'

Lily chats to other guests in the room before skipping back to the kitchen, job done, just in time for the ***Goodbye Song*** with Lunar.

'Thanks Lily,' I say. 'Was everyone all right?'

'No, the fat woman with the red nose asked if you've got a fish knife.'

'Fish knife? What is this – Rick Stein's? It's a kipper fillet, madam!'

'Can you pop these down to her please, darling?' I say, handing her the antique, bone-handled fish cutlery passed down by my grandma. 'Tell her to . . .'

'What?'

'Nothing.'

Going to the cinema was an adventure; and for Lily a trial, since she hated me falling asleep. I did manage to get off for five minutes during ***Cats and Dogs***, but normally she'd spot the signs and give me a prod.

'Dad! Wake up!'

And I was the archetypal panto Dad. Debbie hated pantos but I loved them, so it was easy for me to take up this mantle, spending two hours every Christmas shouting 'behind you' and fighting for the Quality Street chucked at the front rows.

At the Horseshoes, Lily would now sit at the bar supping orange squash, or play in the back garden on the rope swing, stopping occasionally to feed the voracious goat behind the fence – far better attractions than any theme park.

During garden openings, which I continued several times a year (though scrapping the teas which I couldn't manage), Lily would give visitors a garden map, take their entrance money, and help mark up the plant labels.

The day before one opening I'd seen Wake's tractors circling the field behind the cottage. This always had the same effect on me as would, say, the sight of a Vodafone truck with a mobile phone mast trundling across. But to be fair to Wake (who, like me, was a local businessman trying to make a living, albeit he was much richer), and to keep our relationship sweet, I only phoned him if spreading the sludge really *could* affect my interests. On this occasion, with the cabbage smell promising to be the visitors' main memory, I decided a call was in order. As usual, within minutes the tractor abandoned its defecatory doings and disappeared from sight. But this time there was a twist. Half an hour later Wake appeared at the front door, trim as ever, with several four-packs of fromage frais.

'Hello, Paul. Sorry about that. Hope it didn't spoil things,' he said, a little obsequiously.

'Not at all. The garden's open tomorrow, and I wanted things to be right for the visitors.'

'I thought the little 'un might like these,' he said, handing over the packs, about twenty tubs in all. He must have seen Lily as he drove past.

'Oh thanks. You didn't need to –– '

'No-oo, it's no problem at all. I get given them by the Creamery, so she's welcome.'

'Thanks, Lewis.'

Lily tucks into one straight away. She'll have to keep at it though – later, I notice the "use by" date was yesterday.

With the last garden visitors gone, Lily would help collect signs from the road and come with me to the vicarage to give Bill the Vicar his share of the takings. Bill had been very supportive after Debbie and Lily left, someone neutral I could talk to about the future. He became a good friend; we'd meet for a pint, and I'd often be inveigled into his league quiz team where it was always Bill that stood up and challenged answers. The clever clogs was usually right.

His church, Holy Trinity in Minsterley, is renowned for its significant collection of 18th century maidens' garlands, funerary mementos placed on the coffins of young girls (and occasionally boys) who'd led a virginal life. A tradition first recorded in England in 1688, garlands survive in only about a dozen churches, Minsterley's crown-shaped examples having wooden frames, decorated with delicate strips of paper and material.

On a low table in the Mothers' Union corner are photograph albums. One picture labelled **Lily Grace May Costello, 31st May 1998** shows Lily, two and a half, dwarfed between mum and dad in a pretty, yellow christening dress, reaching up for their hands. When it was taken I had no idea that three months later we'd be living apart.

Undoing our marriage was not without wrinkles, but we got on with it sensibly, keeping Lily clear of worry, a significant achievement when you hear about other people's experiences. The way ahead was steady for all of us, and I knuckled down to running the B&B and garden with undiminished passion.

Then Tony stood up and said . . .

···   Tony's Foot-in-Mouth Disease   ···

'Don't go to the countryside!'

The day Tony Blair said this on television, my phone stopped ringing. Thanks for that, Tone, on behalf of countryside Bed and Breakfast proprietors everywhere. Possibly the most loose-tongued statement ever made on national telly; the sort of thing you expect from someone at the back end of a booze-up, which a friend reminds them of next day:

'Oh Gaw-w-d! Tell me you're kidding! I didn't really say that, did I?'

No doubt he meant well; he was just ill advised. Votes count, and with an election looming, politicians were in a cautious mood, treading gently with the farming sector the way they do. If someone was going to pay the price for the outbreak of foot-and-mouth disease in an abattoir in Essex on 19th February 2001 and its rapid spread across the country, it wasn't going to be the abattoir. Or anyone in the farming community. Or Nick Brown, the Agriculture Minister, who condoned the transport of infected cows for slaughter through miles of undiseased territory and wouldn't listen to the vaccination argument. No – it would be the small business sector that took the biggest blow. B&Bs, outdoor equipment shops, village tea rooms, anyone in the countryside depending on visitors for a living.

February was when people made summer plans. Whatever rural ventures they had in mind were switched to cities. Because Tony said so. Well, hooray for cities.

As for Americans, the decision to boycott Britain was a no-brainer. Children's tea sets had nothing on this. At least I saved on wear and tear from fat Americans traipsing through my cottage and on ear plugs trying to block out their fatuous commentary. Takings at The Fat Cafe would definitely plunge.

It's not that I didn't sympathise with farmers whose livelihood was in peril. I'm sure most were fond of their livestock and proud of what they'd achieved. Pictures of burning cow pyres and stories from tear-filled farmers touched me as much as anyone. But the government looked after them. Compensation seemed on offer at a level that would see them okay – often more than.

Many farmers had already diversified, finding secondary sources of income. Some rural B&Bs could also get by, typically where one person ran the B&B and the other had a separate job. But at Cricklewood Cottage there *was* only me, and I depended entirely on visitors.

During the outbreak, each ten seconds of news footage meant one less person phoning. Ironically, I did have some Ministry of Agriculture officials staying to check and cull local livestock, but it wouldn't be enough. With few enquiries coming in, I signed up for Jobseeker's Allowance – Unemployment Benefit in old money.

The process at Shroosbury Job Centre was surprisingly simple. Although Tony and his cronies had tightened up on benefits under the New Deal, and I'd expected a cool reception, I sensed they were under orders to take a soft line on people affected by the outbreak. I'd found myself another source of income.

Around Minsterley, security processes were stepped up. The Creamery had a gang of space-suited disinfectors manning the entrance gates twenty-four hours a day to spray milk tankers, any of which might transmit the disease locally or import it from further afield. Every farm entrance had disinfectant mats for vehicles and troughs for dipping footwear. Ominous signs sprang up on farm gates and footpath entrances, telling people to keep out. Those who chose to ignore Tony's advice not to come and stay at my B&B were subject to tight controls about where they could walk; these adventurous few, who were determined not to have their holidays spoilt, have my undying admiration.

Geoff's family's farm wasn't affected, but some farmers sensed the wind of change and used the compensation to move out of livestock into other forms of farming or property-related activities, like B&B or visitor centres. A few took the profit and carried on. I watched in a Pontesbury pub as a group of ruddy-faced young farmers had a celebratory drink.

'He told me my sheep weren't infected,' said one of them. 'But when I pushed him, he agreed to get rid of them to be on the safe side, ha ha ha!'

'He took all mine,' said another, with a broad smirk. 'They were right as rain, ha ha ha! Good price too. Cheers!'

The air grew so hot around me, my beer started to boil.

The media had a field day – literally. Wherever there was a field there was a camera. Arguably, the media offers advice as well as news – in this case, telling the public which areas were affected and what action to take. Then again, they were always going to milk foot-and-mouth for every upturned udder they could find. The trouble is that footage of burning carcasses implies a continuing problem. With library film used to dramatise the subject, even when an area was officially clear of the disease it would easily trigger rumours of a recurrence, especially on a slow conversation day in the Bridge – or at any time in The States.

The money from the Job Centre was handy, but with summer trade wiped out I needed more. Tony wouldn't pay me indefinitely, and savings put aside from the previous summer had long since gone.

In the end the ill wind did me a favour. In June I got a call from Debbie at Stokesay Castle, saying they had no gardener at the moment, and would I go and spend a few days tidying the overgrown herbaceous borders. I'd learnt to love gardening. Mine had become a delightful retreat for B&B guests and NGS visitors, and helping at Stokesay would be a pleasure.

Being at the same workplace as Debbie was strange at first, but we soon got used to it. I relished the Castle garden, working alongside the public and being paid handsomely for the privilege, and my boss Richard, who managed other English Heritage gardens in the region, liked what I did.

'Would you be willing to do the job permanently?' he asked tentatively at the end of the week.

Had this happened in normal times, ensconced in my country cottage with income arriving on the doorstep, I'd have declined. But foot-and-mouth had questioned my reliance on the B&B, and I now had a real choice.

It had felt good getting away part of the time, so maybe life shouldn't be all about the business.

'I'd love to,' I said, 'as long as I can fit the two days around my B&B.'

So Stokesay it was. As trade picked up, I took advantage of the flexibility Richard allowed, working when it suited me. I could cater for guests at breakfast, service their rooms, go to Stokesay, and be back in time for new arrivals. And I became selective about how many guests I took, choosing never to recapture the heady levels of business from earlier years. For this reason I stopped keeping an annual count of how many people stayed, because comparison with previous years would be false. The record of nine hundred and fifty-four and a half had come in the year Lily was born – 1995, the best year ever. The half came from single people paying less for a room; as geeky a statistic, I suppose, as listing the purchase of individual Mars Bars. Though it meant something to me at the time, I doubt that such precise accounting had contributed much to my matrimonial welfare once things started going wrong.

I wouldn't have wished foot-and-mouth on anyone. But it was a life-changer for many, and certainly reset my future in a way I'd never expected.

If the foot-and-mouth outbreak hadn't been enough to deter Americans, the tragedy of the falling Twin Towers and attack on the Pentagon in September the same year would make sure of it.

Like President Kennedy's assassination, the terrorist attack would be one of those occasions about which people say: 'I remember where I was when I heard the news.' In my case, I'd returned from gardening at Stokesay mid-afternoon to find guests sitting boggle-eyed in front of the television when there'd normally be no-one around. We sat in anguish as the towers collapsed – live. Numbed at the enormity of what was happening, and feeling helpless at such a distance, it was impossible to look away.

It reminded me of other tragic footage, like dead and dying POWs when concentration camps were liberated, and Herbert Morrison's distraught radio commentary as the Hindenburg passenger airship disintegrated in flames above an airport in New Jersey. As much as Americans irritate me, I felt at one with the tear-stricken faces pointing at the burning buildings and running helplessly from the rushing wall of dust as the towers tumbled. Humbling experiences.

··· My Basil's Last Stand ···

Without Sybil as a foil, Basil Fawlty would have been lost. Alone, his rantings would have been the mutterings of an eccentric. He'd either have gone mad – or mellowed.

After Debbie went, my alter ego did lose impetus. But the turning point may have come before that. As with the Twin Towers a few years later, little can match the bonding effect of a disaster in public life, and so it was at Cricklewood Cottage on the morning of 6th September 1997, the day of Princess Diana's funeral.

My full house of six guests wanted to watch it at the cottage before going out for the day. We'd stuck by our policy of not having televisions in bedrooms, believing the noise at night would disturb others, so everyone gathered in the Reading Room. With Lily at nursery Debbie and I joined them, closing the curtains to shut out the reality of everyday life. We fell as one into a reflective mood. There was a mechanical air about the commentary, the coverage strung out by repetition of the route the cortege would take and which politician or member of the Royal Family would do what. But more moving was the look on people's faces as they walked up to add their insignificant bunch to the lake of flowers outside Buckingham Palace, and the silent tears as Princess Di went by.

The box of tissues I left on the coffee table wasn't wasted. The eight of us sobbed our way through the funeral in cinema silence, and at the end when I pulled back the curtains to a bright day, the room emptied and we went about our lives.

Whilst this event no doubt touched My Basil, it wasn't until the foot-and-mouth outbreak forced him to take a second job that he accepted there was more to life than wrangling with customers. Before that, there was still time to score points, and even after he'd dismissed the bikers, other guests gave him plenty of opportunities.

Many of my older visitors are on medication. Breakfast is a common time for taking tablets, which some people keep in plastic containers like dice cups, and others lay loose on the table. One day I spot a man with about two dozen tablets and capsules lying in wait. Yellows and blacks, whites and creams, some the size of an aspirin, others no bigger than a sturgeon egg. They'd make a good game of forfeit in the pub – join them all up to make the word TAB without using the cream ones more than once in a letter. Loser buys the drinks.

'You'll be rattling away after that lot,' I say.

'Sorry?' he says, with a face like a brick.

'I said, we'll hear you coming a mile off.'

'God, you old people. No sense of humour.'

'You have a lot of pills to remember,' I say, digging the hole deeper. 'More toast?'

A British couple call at the cottage, and the woman asks to view the room. Some people like to book accommodation as they go, so I always make sure the rooms are in a ready state. Most casual callers are delighted at chancing on somewhere so tasteful, and unless they overdo it like the gushing Ozzies, I feel flattered at their reaction – undoubtedly one of the feel-good aspects of the job. This particular couple stayed four nights.

John Fothergill didn't approve of such viewing:

'Two rather stodgy underbred folks came and asked for a room, adding – "Can we see it?" I explained as usual that it wasn't necessary to inspect my rooms unless, of course, one was going to stay some time. "Then we can go elsewhere," rang out the harsh voice of the woman. " "You can," I said, "and so relieve the situation," and out they went. I'm rather tired of this unpleasantness; next time I shall make them pay for the inspection.'

But Cricklewood Cottage doesn't suit everyone. I show some Dutch people the Bow Room, a small double with a large en suite.

'We were hoping for a little more room to spread out,' says the woman, through what sounds like surplus phlegm at the back of her throat.

'But you have a beautiful cottage, and thanks for showing us,' says the man, his attitude as impeccable as his English.

'Good luck to you. There's nothing else up the valley. It's Utterly Undiscovered, you know.'

Two Belgians, speaking little English, inspect the Rose Room. They pull back the bed linen, peer inside the shower cubicle, bounce on the bed, check the views and poke about on the tea tray. I half expect them to nibble the garibaldis. All the while, they pass comments in Flemish (so that's where "phlegm" comes from), none of which I understand. I feel like a spare part – like I'm having my case searched by a Customs Officer looking for a stash that doesn't exist whilst pretending I'm not there.

'Erm, can I get you a stethoscope to check for life behind the plasterboard?'

'Okay,' says the man, with a pleasant smile.

'Yes?' I say, sticking to words that cross languages. It's only a matter of time before one of us says "good".

'Goot,' he says, inching closer to a decision. 'My . . .' he says, pointing first at his wife then the en suite.

'Good,' I say, at which point she disappears into the bathroom and bolts the door. To save embarrassment I wait downstairs.

'Can I help with the luggage?' I say, at the front door, mimicking a milkmaid and speaking loudly with exaggerated vowels to help get the message across.

'No – okay,' he says, holding up his hands like a policeman stopping a car at a road block.

I wait for them to fetch their cases, preparing my welcome spiel, or at least a mimed version. But in vain. After five minutes I check the car park and find it empty.

'A thank you would have been nice, if you just wanted my toilet,' says My Basil, shaking his fist down the road. *'Where were you in the war, eh?'*

Fothergill would have been proud of me:

'It may seem petty to bother about this sort of thing, but we Innkeepers pay for our lavatories and should not tolerate these sneaking attempts to get privilege and shy retirement for nothing.'

I charge £25 each a night for a double, the going rate round here. When we started it was £9, the increase reflecting inflation and what the B&B is worth.

'That's a bit steep,' says a woman on the phone.

'You'll find it the same elsewhere.'

'We only paid £15 earlier this year.'

'I don't know anywhere round here that does it for that.'

'Well it might have been somewhere else – but nevertheless . . .'

Maybe she's used to staying in places like Torquay or Blackpool where the supply of back-to-back B&Bs, established in the 50s and 60s during the post-war boom for seaside holidays, far exceeds today's demand. Competition for customers means that all roads into these resorts have boards advertising identical facilities at the lowest price:

> *Yet Another Guest House*
> *Hot and Cold Water*
> *Tea and Coffee. TV   £15*

I can never understand why they don't mention beds. I'd have thought they were pretty important too.

'Sounds a bit much to me,' the woman says.

'Well, I *do* have a room free, and that's the rate. Would you like me to hold it for you?'

'Not at that price.'

'If money's the problem, try Shroosbury campsite, madam.'

'Can you do it any cheaper?'

'I'd rather drive six inch nails into my head.'

'I'm afraid not. I'm very busy.'

'I'll leave it then.'

'You misunderstood, madam. I meant I'd rather drive six inch nails into my head than have you stay in my house at any price.'

'Not a problem. Goodbye.'

The single supplement also causes grief. With three double rooms from which to make a living, a part-occupied room can leave me short. Yet it doesn't seem fair or commercially sensible to charge full room price for one person, particularly if business is slow. Accustomed to single travel, I appreciate this. A loading of fifty per cent is a fair compromise, especially if they're on business and can claim it back. In winter, when there's less demand, I might waive any supplement, whereas at peak times like the Flower Show I offer no reduction at all. Supply and demand.

'Why's that?' asks a man, when I quote £37. 50.

'Because I'm a small business and need to make a living.'

'That doesn't seem very fair.'

'Fair? It's your choice to ride a poxy bike from John O'Groats to Land's End. Do you think I'm a charity or something?'

'I'm doing the ride for Cancer Research.'

'Okay, you can have it for £25.'

What is it about people who can't read? I have very few signs in the house, but guests ignore those I *do* have. "Private" seems clear to me. My dictionary says:

'Not open to or available for the general use of the public.'

'Morning!'

The broken egg in my frying pan spreads rapidly across the pristine Teflon surface. After more than ten years I've got egg-frying down to a fine art, only to have an intruder make me jump and ruin it.

'Can't you read? You've walked straight past a "Private" sign and made me break my egg.'

'Can I help you?' I say.

'Yes, we're running late. Would nine o'clock be okay instead of eight thirty?'

'That's fine.'

Fothergill would've had him. Weary of living amongst 'arrogant and grasping half-breds', his take on two people who turned up late was:

'Two zoological specimens to dinner – naturally I hated the sight of them,' though he couldn't do enough for the couple when he recognised the man as playwright J M Barrie.

An elderly man brushes past a "Private" sign to change his wife's order from fried to scrambled egg.

'Not a problem,' I say. 'Just one egg?'

They've stayed before, and he's a nice old man. It's only as he shuffles back towards the Sun Room that I realise why he's shuffling. Trapped round his left leg is a small handbag with long leather straps.

'Excuse me, Mr Murdoch, you've got something caught on your leg.'

'Yes, my wife put it there to make sure I came back,' he says, laughing.

Whilst I accept that marriage is a binding agreement, I'm not sure that attaching a weight to your husband's leg is quite in the spirit of the thing. Seems more like slavery.

'Why? Does she think you might run off?'

'Yes – I got five numbers plus the bonus on Saturday, and the cheque will be in my name.'

I'd heard a discussion on Radio 4 about the word "literally". Whatever its original meaning, the word was now being used so freely as to make a nonsense of it. Sports commentators were worst.

At the Wimbledon Finals: 'The crowd's going mad; the roof's literally caving in.'

At a Premiership soccer match: 'What a shocking tackle. He's literally taken the defender's legs off.'

And a celebrity talking about adopting siblings from Africa had a sad tale: 'They literally had to split the children in two.'

The woman from the Tulip Room says she has an apology to make. I get used to this preface to what usually turns out to be something trivial, like a pipette of coffee on the duvet cover or a soap mark on the floor.

'I've cracked the bedroom sink.'

'Right. When you say cracked . . .'

'There's now a hole in it. I dropped a perfume bottle. It must have hit the sink at just the right angle.'

'Just the right angle? Were you aiming it then, madam?'
My main concern is that if it's irreparable I've got to do something about it today, like when Kimberley the fat American broke my bed. And these are period hand basins, so it would take a while finding the right one.
'Okay, I'll come and have a look. Don't worry – these things happen.'
'You just can't get the customers these days.'
'I'm so sorry – it literally flew out of my hand.'
'Madam, if you keep on about it, you're going to drive me mad – literally. Oh.'

⋯ Fur Coated Visitors ⋯

One day a mole finds his way through the open back door into the kitchen. His large, two-thumbed paws, ideal for ripping my lawn to pieces, are not so good for a quick getaway, so I easily corner him on the steps to the Sun Room. And there he starts screaming like a child in distress. Had there been anyone else in the cottage they'd have dialled 999. Sensing my hand he screeches louder, throwing his barrelled body at the fingers with immense power. I see how a solitary mole can do so much damage overnight, and I'm glad I've never had to pick a live one out of a trap.

As I nudge Mr Mole into a Tupperware container, for some reason he stops crying. I could strike a mortal blow, but having years ago put one of Debbie's sick rabbits out of its misery with the back of a spade, succeeding only after a dozen gruesome lunges, I'd vowed never again to be so barbaric. Instead I drive him a mile up a country lane and free him under the hedge of a young farmer who'd conned the Ministry of Agriculture in the foot-and-mouth outbreak.

'There must be twenty moles under that field, Mr Inspector. Some looked a bit dodgy. Any chance of, er . . . ?'

'No problem, sir. We'll dig up the field and burn all of them. Good rate for moles. Any other wildlife we can compensate you for, sir?'

Re-stocking his mole population was the least I could do.

'Paul, quick!' Debbie had called from the Sun Room one day. 'A squirrel with no tail,' she said, pointing down the garden at the creature trotting along a bench.

'It's a rat,' I said, not mentioning the evidence I'd seen under the shed and in the compost. It reminded me of the rat Manuel was conned into buying from a pet shop as a Filigree Siberian hamster, and how Fawlty spent the whole episode trying to keep it away from Mr Carnegie, the Health Inspector.

'A rat?' said Debbie. 'Good God, we've got rats!'

Strange how that word raises so much fear. Had I said it was a rare, smooth-haired, lesser-pooping Shropshire squirrel she'd have tried stroking it or offering acorns. But rats? We were doomed!

Conditioned to thinking only city sewers and back-alley squalor attracted vermin, our idea of wildlife was squirrels scurrying up trees, red deer grazing at the edge of verdant forests and buzzards floating on warm currents off the Stiperstones – all to the background music of some Beatrix Potter movie.

Buzzards there certainly were. Thriving in ideal terrain, their faint miaowing and graceful spirals drawing the eye, they ventured closer each year, especially in winter when foraging in the hills was less fruitful. Near the back door one morning I find a giant specimen perched on a post checking the brookside grass for signs of a decent meal. Disturbed from his vigil, he turns and stares long enough for me to get a rare close-up of his sharp eyes and iron beak, the tools of a survivor.

Of course there are plenty of squirrels, and as well as common garden birds we have goldcrests in the conifers, crying curlews each spring in Geoff's field and dippers, herons and grey wagtails using the brook. And in summer it's a joy watching tiny pipistrelle bats criss-crossing the garden after sunset for their staple meal of moths and mosquitoes.

What we hadn't thought was that it was also a perfect setting for the squatters of the animal kingdom – mice, moles, shrews, voles and squirrels without tails, or Swots as we called them. Water is a favourite habitat, and the overgrown banks make a fantastic refuge. If Jack was right about the human contribution to the brook, there'd also be a plentiful food supply. And across the water the field is a safe haven, especially if corn or barley is grown, offering food and shelter for much of the year.

Swots visit intermittently. It's as if they prefer moving around – Romany Swots, perhaps. They don't come near the cottage, so don't prove a threat to health or hygiene. The compost heap is a great hangout for Swots and mice, especially in winter – warm, nutritious and safe. Apart from one occasion when a Swot flew over my shoulder as I removed the corrugated-iron lid, leaving me as shaken as *it* must have been, the only give-away is a neat entrance hole.

I spend glorious hours managing the twin compost bins. Five feet high and three feet wide, each made from timber and corrugated iron salvaged from the barn, I fill them with anything that breaks down – kitchen refuse, shredded newspaper, Hoover bags, plant trimmings, wood shavings, bonfire ash and recycled earth. Layered every few inches as an activator is the fresh cow manure I buy from Geoff.

Each bin takes a year to fill. When it will take no more, I turn the contents into the second bin, clambering on top with fork and wellies, happy as a child in a sandpit. Tiny mice scurry away, and the flash of electric blue is a slow worm panicking in the sudden daylight. Once transferred, the covered mixture reduces to a friable, black tilth in six months, ready for layering on flower beds or for potting up plants. Compost – one of nature's wonders.

Jack said urine was a good additive. I did wonder why Violet used to amble up their garden with such regularity, but hadn't liked to ask. Personally, I've not sprayed my compost, but I do mention it to friends who use my tent rather than pay for a room.

'Wee on my compost if you like,' I say. 'Save you coming up to the house in the dark. I've left some wellies for you.'

'I'd rather not,' says Carol from Chester, giving me a strange look.

'Tell you what,' I say, 'if you wee on the compost I'll throw in breakfast. Indoors I mean, not on the heap.'

'Hm. Including mushrooms and fried bread?'

'Of course! I'm not mean, you know!'

'And two eggs?'

'Two eggs? Hm. Oh, all right, two eggs.'

'Okay – deal!'

I don't tell her about the rats.

Moles come and go too. Romany moles. When they arrive it's like an army has invaded, though it's normally a lone explorer. I wage war with Mr Mole. I don't need another range of hills – the Stiperstones are fine. Although we'd sacrificed a lot of grass for Jack's playing fields and made gorgeous flower borders in its place, the idea was to keep the rest as lawn. If Mr Mole chose to build castles and dungeon-runs in the borders, fine. But in the lawn – let battle commence.

It can drag on for days. To make up for their poor eyesight the suspicious creatures have an extraordinary sense of smell and a strong instinct telling them something's not right. To stay friendly with the NSPCM (National Society for the Prevention of Cruelty to Moles), I started with humane deterrents – a child's plastic windmill stuck in a hillock or a greetings card delivered first class to the entry hole. I was especially hopeful with a card from the "Moles" section in my local Spar (just under "Granddaughter's Birthdays"), saying:

> *Hello Mr Mole.*
> *I love you. But please go away. Or else.*

'You do realise moles don't understand English, and probably can't see it anyway?' Debbie said.

I hadn't thought of that. And having also failed to discourage the little dears with a slow release gas cartridge, I resort to Jack's country recipe:

INGREDIENTS
One stout wooden stick
Galvanised-iron spring traps from local farm merchants
One pair well-used garden gloves
Large leaves – foxgloves etc
METHOD
Push stick firmly into raised grass until it goes in without resistance
Repeat in same area to determine direction of run
Excavate neat hole in run, putting turf to one side
Set trap and lower into run, wearing gloves to mask human smell
Place pieces of turf and leaf around trap handles to block out light
The trap now forms part of the run
Set remaining traps in other areas
Check daily to see if traps have been sprung (handles will be released)

It's hit-and-miss, but always hit in the end. At first the canny fellow teases me, switching burrows, starting new ones or pushing soil ahead to trigger the finely poised trap. But eventually he gets careless. Finding the slain invader means I've rescued my lawn. Fair cop – I did try to warn him off. But the victory is hollow. It seems sad that a velvety, perfectly-proportioned, underground powerhouse should have to meet such a sticky end.

The most persistent vermin are mice. By mice I mean anything small, brown and furry – field mice, bank voles and shrews with pointy noses which, just to confuse everyone, David Attenborough of the BBC (the television one) calls shroos not shrose.

Few buildings are sealed, least of all old ones. Jack's bungalow has more holes than wall, and our cottage too has many secret doorways. Mice can squeeze their soft bodies through a half inch hole. They are capable of breeding after fifty days and the gestation period is twenty, with an average litter of ten. Present all year round, they **breed** all year round. That's a lot of mice. And most of them love my house. We'd realised there was a problem when we first arrived, listening to the nightly scurrying of tiny feet in the ceiling space above the living room and the crackling of what turned out to be a Smiths crisps bag being shredded for a nest.

As fields are harvested and the temperature drops, any creature in its right mind tries to find a warmer home. The rooms at the back of the cottage are single storey – the Sun Room, the kitchen and Lily's room – and it's in the roof space above these that the mice arrive for their winter holiday. I love seeing pointy-nosed shrews and marble-eyed mice foraging in flower beds or the banks of the brook; that's sweet country life. But enter my patch and, like moles, they're fair game.

Apart from hygiene issues, the idea of sharing the cottage with these fur-coated fellows might, we'd thought, be difficult to sell to visitors. No doubt I could have found a positive spin as Fothergill did when he discovered that 'rats overrun the house':

'Yesterday a girl came screaming down the stairs from the lavatory calling out "There's a rat, there's a rat!", and fell into the arms of her young man waiting below in the hall, who tenderly folded her to himself – for the first time as it looked to me. She had indeed done well to sustain the rat emotion so long and use it so opportunely.'

All the back rooms have a loft hatch. Inside each I set the only effective remedy, Little Nipper mouse traps, which I check daily to ensure the bait is intact and the traps are unsprung. Jack taught me to use butter not cheese because the clever darlings knock cheese off and carry it away. Rats are even cleverer. I once baited rat traps (Big Nippers) in the shed with bacon rind. For months the rind disappeared and the traps were never sprung. I gave up when I found a note saying:

> *Thanks for the bacon.*
> *We're moving on now – you know us Romany rats.*
> *PS: Rubbish traps, son! PPS: We prefer Danepak.*

I clear scores of mice from the traps every year. They never get further than my tempting nugget of New Zealand Anchor, leaving the lived-in parts of the cottage all clear. Predators probably catch the same amount again, and a few escape, sometimes taking the traps with them. But with Mother Nature at work they multiply as fast as I can lay the traps. And killing them is as unrewarding as catching moles. A tiny shrew squashed in a trap ten times its size is a sad sight, and removing mice carcasses is an unpleasant pastime, second only to rodding a drain. They decay very quickly.

Note to self: find a greetings card with instructions in mole Braille.

⋯ Ups and Downs ⋯

The clumping lasted five seconds, then silence. It was like a muted drum roll reverberating through the cottage, with a stifled squeal to each beat.

I'm pretty sure what it is. I picture a woman rolling raggedly down a steep flight of stairs in a black and white murder movie, and lying crooked at the bottom as she mutters clues that no-one will hear. Then I find Mrs Moody, an elderly lady from Weymouth, slumped at the foot of the stairs to the Rose Room.

'She's fallen,' says her husband, gently coaxing her up.

'Are you okay?' I say, tamely. I feel helpless and for some reason guilty – in nearly as much shock as she is.

'I came down on my back,' she says. 'I missed the top step and felt myself going.'

'I think she's all right,' says Mr Moody, 'but we'll go to the hospital just in case.'

I'm relieved to see no crumpled limbs. She gradually regains composure and climbs to her feet. Declining my offer to call an ambulance, the man guides her to their car where she lowers herself onto the front seat, inch by wincing inch.

In the event nothing is broken, just bad bruising. The gentle couple were more upset about the five hours in Accident and Emergency. When the triage nurse spotted her entering upright and breathing, Mrs Moody was guaranteed a long wait. Emerging at six o'clock after tests, one day of their weekend had been lost.

My fear of American-style litigation proves unwarranted. But each day has me dreaming up elaborate courtroom scenarios, and it's months before I stop checking the fittings on that staircase. Had it been a fat American taking the quick way down amidst a flurry of suitcases, I'd have been sued for everything I own. I applaud the Moodys for their true British grit.

This was one of several awkward incidents after I started running the B&B alone. Dealing with difficult situations goes with the territory, but it helps having someone to share them with, not only for practical purposes but to talk through personal concerns. Debbie had been good at this. But with only friends or neighbours around, I felt more vulnerable. Though it could have been a lot worse, my subsequent obsession with checking the stairs showed how much Mrs Moody's fall touched me; someone close might have helped me get over it quicker.

There were weird people. A New Zealand guy called Barry talked to himself endlessly.

'Now what shall I have? Cornflakes, I think. There's the milk. Not too much. Don't want to drown it. Sugar's on the table.'

'Pardon?' I said, walking past, outside the Sun Room.

'Nothing,' said Barry, carefully guiding his bowl towards the table.

'Sorry – wondered if I could help.'

'Could go into Shroosbury today. Might take the bus. Better check the timetable. Could ask Paul. Have you got a timetable, Paul?'

'Yeah, sure. I'll bring it through.'

'Thanks. Here's my table. Good – radio's on. Listen to the news. See what's going on. Sit down now.'

I leave him to mix with the other guests. He's harmless enough – just another customer. And there'll be no shortage of conversation – he's great for breaking the ice.

And there were situations more irritating than threatening, but awkward in the sense that I had to confront guests. Like the people who used the white room kettle as a teapot to brew their tea, leaving the inside of it estuary brown. And the couple in the Tulip Room which had no bath tub, who snuck into the unoccupied Bow Room which did, to have a good soak.

'I don't believe it! Whose house is *this?'*

Good initiative, but they never asked me, never told me, and didn't clear up afterwards. So when I showed the room to a new guest shortly afterwards, we discovered the dirt ring together.

'No Mrs Batsmel, I didn't leave the scum line and curly hair for your personal pleasure.'

Admittedly, I put aside my indignation when I found the generous tip the bathtub trespassers had left in their room. Guilt money. And I did let off a couple of blokes whom I found using my kitchen, since they'd become reliable visitors for the quiet month of February, attending the annual Bridge Convention in Telford. Their match times were erratic, and it smoothed the way if they could make toast for themselves or get milk from the fridge.

The experience that touched me most was when David came to stay. What happened with him was not of my making, but because he was staying under my roof I felt partly responsible, and sharing things afterwards with Geoff proved a blessing.

I come under pressure from Shropshire Social Services to put up a client needing respite from a domestic problem, a man who lives nearby, which may account for my B&B being targeted. I tend to push away corporate business since they usually pay on receipt of invoice and make me wait months for the money. As a small Bed and Breakfast I prefer cash trade and a deposit for advance bookings – it's amazing how that stops people cancelling at the last moment or not showing up.

'Sorry, I can't make it. I think I might have flu coming,' they'd say.

'Madam, do you mean flu is heading your way – like a tornado? Or have you actually got it?'

I'm given little information by Social Services, but it seems that a farmer is in financial difficulty, affecting his marriage. The Council asks me to put him up for a week or so while he continues working on the farm by day.

At first I refuse, foreseeing delays in payment and not wanting to get involved in someone else's problems. But my twelve years with Social Services in Sussex, albeit in administration, had not left me untouched, and the social worker persuades me to see the human side. She also guarantees speedy payment, good in November with few other guests. I'm finally convinced by the man's being local, realising that on another occasion it could be me. "Do unto thy neighbour . . . "

With a changed name, David comes to stay Monday through Friday. He's a timid chap with a gentle smile, eager to please. I try to be extra understanding but still treat him as a paying guest, which in a way he is. He likes his room and enjoys the warmth of the cottage after being out in raw autumn weather. He skips breakfast, works long hours, and eats out at night. I see little of him, but all seems well.

On Wednesday evening of the second week David returns earlier than usual. The cottage goes quiet and, sensing it's different from other days, I start to worry. After an hour the thought of a man upstairs, possibly depressed, gets too much for me. Tiptoeing up, I hear a low moan through the wall like someone trapped under rubble. I fear the worst, wondering what I might have to do before the ambulance arrives.

'Are you all right in there?' I say through the door, softly.

The moaning stops.

'Hello,' I say a little louder. 'Is everything okay?'

'What? What's that?' comes a muffled reply.

'Sorry, didn't mean to disturb you. I wondered if there's anything you needed.'

'It's all right. I fell asleep in the bath; must have been dreaming,' he calls out cheerfully, putting my mind at rest. Later I apologise for intruding, and he is kind and forgiving about it.

After two weeks David leaves. I get a cheque from the Council, and feel glad I waived my cash-in-hand attitude for someone whose life is not quite as good as mine.

A few days later Geoff pulls up on his tractor when he sees me in the front garden. He knew David, not as a friend or through business but on the farming grapevine. He says he'd seen him going in and out of the cottage but hadn't liked to say anything to me because David's situation was rife with rumour.

He also tells me David was found yesterday, in another farmer's field, hanging from an oak tree.

··· A Singular Experience ···

Unless they're a disciple of Howard Hughes, few people enjoy being entirely on their own for prolonged periods. Radio and TV offer airwave companionship and mask the silence of an empty house, but the company of other people, those you know and those you haven't yet met, is a nagging attraction.

On a comfort scale of one to ten, I've always been about eight point five living alone – nine point five on a good day, and ten on a "stuff the world" one. Throughout university and for several years after, even when I had a girlfriend and a circle of mates, I was happy spending long periods on my own. I'd hitch-hike alone round the UK and Europe, taking odd jobs to keep me going. From washing cars in Cardiff to bar work in a Country House Hotel in Blairgowrie, run by a nymphomaniac woman and her gay husband who ironically spent half his time in Brighton. From picking hops in Kent to cutting and stacking dried, salt-cod in the Norwegian Lofoten Islands inside the Arctic Circle, the two smelliest jobs I've ever had, disastrous if you were going out on the town that night.

Moving about suited my temperament. I liked its randomness – trying different things, visiting new places, meeting whoever crossed my path and *always* having something interesting to talk about – a colourful life portfolio. Whether it was in my blood or a reaction to the routine I'd rejected as a teenager, I'd only have to be home a few weeks before I felt the need to go off somewhere new. My Drift drifted on.

Even within marriage I enjoyed being away or out for the day by myself from time to time, especially if travel was involved. I've always liked travelling singly, though holidays with loved ones have their proper place too. After each marriage breakdown, the excitement and freedom of planning my life itinerary had far exceeded any dejection at being alone.

But being human, I have that underlying desire to be sociable, and that's what I faced after Debbie and Lily left. Lily was my top priority but I needed adult friendship too. And whilst I wasn't looking for a one-to-one relationship, and certainly not a live-in one, there were moments when I yearned to share things with someone special, a woman whose expectations were perhaps as unconventional as mine.

In earlier life, friendships and relationships developed through work, and before that, school or university. But my home was now my work. I was unlikely to make friends or start relationships with customers at Cricklewood Cottage and it might have been professionally unsound to try. So here I was, in an isolated country setting, needing to get out and establish a new life.

Easier said than done. Going to the pub and visiting friends outside the area was a palliative for the first year, but it wasn't the answer. My life in Shropshire had been built around the B&B, a small circle of friends, and now Lily. Our friends had included Debbie's NCT pals, but pleasant though they were, as a single man my agenda didn't match theirs. And my solo socialising for the last ten years – going to the pub and taking short breaks – had been to get away from domestic routines, not to create a secondary social group or find another woman.

In a scattered rural population dominated by agriculture, there seemed little chance of meeting the right kind of person. There were no social organisations to speak of, unless I wanted to do yoga with Minsterley women at the Parish Hall on a Thursday. It was like finding the supermarket shelves under-stocked and the items on your list not available.

I'd never fancied newspaper dating columns, or Lonely Hearts as they're known, an unfortunate title since it puts everyone into the same pot – a homogeneous bunch of desperate no-hopers or mad people. Apart from being like a job application (which I'm no good at) with hundreds of people applying, it's a remote mechanism lacking credibility.

"Bubbly curvaceous blonde seeks honest gentleman for companionship and good times – and wherever else it may lead. "

Yeah, right.

The same applies to the new vogue for internet dating, and with no computer I was ill-equipped to deal with that anyway.

Come the new millennium I decided it was time for a fresh push. Scouring the papers, I spotted a small ad in the Shroosbury Chronicle for a club for single people with the imaginative title of Friday Night Club (FNC), and thought I'd give it a go. The instructions from the lady on the phone took me to the car park of Morris's Lubricants in the trading estate at the back of Shroosbury station. Wondering if I'd got the right place, I negotiated the car round high stacks of oil drums silhouetted in the dark, and parked up near the small, back door entrance.

Nonchalantly joining the check-in queue, as if I had a lifetime's experience of this sort of thing, I gave my name and address and one pound fifty to a brittle-looking woman with upright hair sat in a cubicle full of coat racks and hangers, beyond which was a dark cavernous room normally used for conferences and training. Desperately needing a pint of anything, and another, but knowing my security for the evening was the option to drive away if I didn't like it, I settled for an orange juice and lemonade, and shuffled off towards the round, twelve-seater tables. If this had been a conference, and the room brightly lit with water jugs and tumblers, and everyone had tidy name badges and an agenda, I'd have felt at home, ready to trigger conversation with the delegate lucky enough to sit next to me. Right now, I sensed it was going to be a long, dry evening.

On the opposite side of my sparsely occupied table, too far away to speak to, were two people of indeterminate sex – not hermaphrodites as such, just it was too dark to tell. I sat alone, rehearsing the opening gambit I might use once someone was close enough.

'Do you come here often?' No – they might have heard that before.

'Is this your first time?' No – they might think it a bit forward, or pervy.

'Hello-oo – is there anybody there?' No – they might think I'm taking the piss, or ill.

I feel more alone than before I arrived. There's something end-of-wedding about the place – a handbag and a couple of half-pint tumblers looking lost on the white table cloths, and a scattering of folk who've run out of conversation and aren't sure when to leave. From what I've seen, there are four women to every man. That perks me up but it also feels unnatural, even threatening. At least the apparent age range of thirty-five to fifty suits me, and there are plenty arriving.

'If I come again, I must get here later,' I think.

After a few conversational skirmishes, I'm escorted to the dance floor by a posse of women, thankfully more gentle than Downy and her mates all those years ago. The group dancing seems very jolly. The ageing DJ works the crowd, emptying the floor with progressively undanceable stuff then fostering a surge from the tables with a winning song. Since you can't see or hear properly, conversation is fraught. I come away from the club with *Dance the Night Away* by the Mavericks ringing through my head, to which we'd all joined in the chorus. By golly, I had a darn good time.

At home I feel like, well, I've just been to a wedding – only I'm far too sober. The party's over, men and women alike have done their "dad at the disco" routine, and everyone was nice to everyone else. Yet I'm not sure a wedding is what I wanted.

I try it again two weeks later, this time hamming it up in the queue and strutting between tables and dance floor – after all, I'm an old-stager now. But I can tell it's not for me. I'm glad I made the effort, but though friendly, the women were not my type. They reminded me of the ones behind the delicatessen counter at Tesco, especially the woman who worked the meat slicer on a Saturday morning, and the cheese lady on a Tuesday. And the atmosphere was functional and contrived – a bit like a wedding, I suppose.

It put me off this kind of set-up for a while. But out of the experience had come two tips I followed up later in the year. A safe topic of conversation had been singles organisations – clubs, holiday companies, hotels and so on. Stemming from this, I treated myself to a picture-postcard Christmas break in Austria with a company called Just You, which specialised in people travelling alone, many of whom were more my type. And I also found out about other singles clubs in the area – and so discovered Network.

Unlike the drink-chat-dance formula of the FNC, Network was an events based organisation run by a charming woman called Sylvie from her home near Shroosbury. The age range and woman-man ratio was similar to FNC, and by now I realised this must always be the case; compared with pubs and night clubs, which women prefer not to visit alone, organised clubs like this are a safe place for them to go.

Sylvie advertised discreetly in the Shropshire Star, and was careful who she accepted. She ran a full itinerary of social events, from hill walks to pub dinners, quiz evenings to Sunday afternoon boules or a jazz club in town. With regular parties in her own home, there was something for everyone. A list was circulated monthly, specifying events and prices, and you sent a cheque for those you wanted to take part in.

It worked. Sylvie ran Network like a mother hen, making sure nobody felt left out or spoilt it for others. The arrangements were safe, and there was no pressure to perform or match up with another person. It was promoted simply as a friendship club. That's not to say that matching didn't take place, but it happened in a natural way and not in a dim conference room yelling frenziedly over Ricky Martin's *Livin' La Vida Loca.*

As well as things I knew I liked, such as a pub meal or a walk on the Long Mynd, I tried things I'd not done before like archery and ice skating. Sometimes the socialising carried on outside Network, a few of us meeting at Bayley's Bar in Shroosbury which had great bands on a Friday night. Network was good for me; at last I was building a life of my own, broadening my social circle and meeting like-minded people.

But everything has its time, and after a year or so the set-up started feeling predictable. There was an added problem that I'd found myself acting as a kind of counsellor. By now I knew that membership of singles clubs was largely made up of people coming out of failed relationships, often following a dramatic break-up. That's not to say there weren't widowed people and some who'd had a limited social life and wanted to do more; and in exceptional cases, people who were alone in the sense that their partners had long-term degenerative illnesses like Parkinsons. But the vast majority, especially women, arrived on the back of a bad separation.

I hated seeing people sitting alone at their first event while others chatted safely on the other side of the room, so I'd always make a personal effort to include them. But having had a relatively calm separation myself, it became onerous soaking up other people's dramas, especially if my encouraging words were taken as romantic interest. While I could appreciate the underlying emotions, I felt awkward when women made this assumption merely because I was talking to them.

Before trying singles clubs, I'd realised they were the butt of many a joke; sadly, the jokes about married men infiltrating them *are* sometimes true, though at Network, Sylvie usually spotted the culprits and removed them straight away. But the public image didn't put me off. As a place for meeting people they are no different from the average night club or office party. It just so happens that everyone is single and for some reason hasn't got the same social life as couples or groups, so clubs give them a chance to find one.

I found Network women as attractive as any I'd met elsewhere, and I did make new friends of both sexes. But whether man or woman, anyone who tried too hard became less attractive, feeding the "lonely and desperate" label attached to single life. And there were those women who might appear positive until the trauma of break-up returned, or depression or menopause held sway. Much as I sympathised, I was trying to forge a healthy social life and didn't need added problems.

But having been without a partner for four years I was at risk of being flattered into a relationship too easily. I needed to be on my guard, or I might end up with a woman with, say, a mad streak. Or anger management problems. Or obsessions. Life was stable, and I didn't need it stirring up.

Yet a clever woman could work out what attracted me, wave her wand, and close the sale. And you know what they say about salesmen . . .

⋯ Caught Napping ⋯

I've always liked a daytime snooze. Lunchtime and late afternoon are favourites, but any time will do. I remember revising for A-levels at home and dropping off with my head on the book soon after I'd started, at ten in the morning. Then there were my two o'clock snoozes at the Council; I'd arrange the desk and chair so that with chin in one hand and pen in the other, it looked like I was really busy. If Slithery Seltzer or one of my Personnel Assistants came in, the door disturbed me and I could gather myself in time.

Driving can be a problem. If I'm travelling a long way I allow extra time for breaks. Once I'm hitting the "wall", and I've pulled off the road, sleep is instant and deep, and I wake up fully refreshed, safe to continue the journey. For some reason, maybe obsession, I make a mental note of the time I shut my eyes and check it again when I awake. The length of nap is always twenty-five to thirty minutes.

My body demands frequent sleep. My old school friend Bill is much the same, but with an extra trick. At a late-night curry, when he's had his fill, his head slowly lowers towards the plate, meeting the residual slurry of pilau rice and chicken madras head on, so to speak. I imagine the six pints of Harveys bitter beforehand has something to do with it. After five minutes he'll wake up, give his turmeric-tipped nose a cursory wipe with the back of his hand, and finish the food as if nothing had happened. I still look forward to Bill's cabaret on return trips to Brighton.

My dad had lunchtime napping down to a fine art. As soon as he'd finished his Welsh rarebit and piece of fruit, his eyes would flicker and he'd be sure to miss the second half of the One o'clock News. Perhaps there's a genetic connection, because I often drop off between one and two. As with driving, I think of it as "recovery sleep", stoking body and mind for the coming hours.

People say I might have narcolepsy. Some of the symptoms fit, but the sleep pattern is erratic, and I'm able to control it. I may go a full week without a nap or have several naps a day, especially if I'm short on sleep or have a hangover. And I've never dropped my head into a bowl of curry – maybe a double chilli-burger, once.

If I'm prevented from falling asleep by, say, the phone ringing or someone disturbing me, I get tetchy.

'Dad! Wake up!'

Between the ages of five and ten, Lily felt insecure if I fell asleep. Poking me awake wasn't to impart some vital piece of information, but sheer panic that I wasn't there to look after her. It took guile to work round this. The darkness of a cinema had potential, but at home, as in the office, I had to think of cunning ruses, like facing the opposite way as I closed my eyes, or wearing dark glasses. Sadly, my sneaky plan was usually exposed by snuffling and snorting as soon as I went off.

'I'm just having a little doze, Lily. Let me sleep.'

'No, dad. You can't!'

'Why not?' I say, blearily.

'Because it's not sleep time. Wake up, dad!' she says, giving me a Mike Tyson to the ribs.

I can fall asleep anywhere. Public transport is a favourite – the rhythm of a train or the sway of a bus, and no fear of crashing. The rushing sound on a plane is good, and the chugging of the engine deep down in a cross-Channel ferry. The London Tube, best on the Circle Line.

Warm doctors' and dentists' waiting rooms. Laid back on the dentist's chair, with a drill whining. Someone Hoovering next door. Launderettes. Two o'clock at conferences (the graveyard shift) – when the whole room nods off, including the speaker. Cinema and theatre, meaning I lose the plot. At a concert. Having tea in a cafe, especially after too long in hot shops or trekking round a museum.

In church. In front of the telly, of course. On a park bench. Reading. In the Departure Lounge at an airport. Lying in the sun. I can even fall asleep standing up at a crowded football match, propped up by those around me.

It was great when I started working for myself. In my own home I could sleep whenever I liked. Guests were rarely around by day and Debbie was often at work. Although it was harder with Lily there, when she was tiny I could usually take a swift nap to coincide with her afternoon sleep.

Once I was living on my own the scope was even greater. Lunchtime was a certainty, recovering from domestic routines and shopping, and following an afternoon working in the garden I could drop off for half an hour on the sofa or in a hot bath. Even on gardening days with English Heritage I could snooze at lunchtime in the folded-back seat of the car.

'Don't you think it's a waste of time, all that sleep?' people say.

'No – it's wonderful. My idea of heaven!'

And a nap in the bath is a strong possibility right now, after rolling huge boulders along the bed of the brook to their final resting place. I've been repairing the dry-stone wall that protects the bog garden from flood damage. Heavy work, but splashing through the shallow, fast-flowing water amongst overhanging ash and sycamore and the smell of leafy earth is pure pleasure. The dipper flashes past, heading for its nest. Screeching magpies, high in the trees, frighten blackbirds into submission, the prize a tasty egg or young chick. A darting movement around my wellies is a rainbow trout looking for pickings from the silt I've disturbed. The setting is as idyllic today as fourteen years ago when we first saw this small roadside cottage crying out for tender loving care.

A storm has been threatening for some while. Indoors the air is tight and the rooms prematurely dark. Something nasty is on its way.

The soothing sounds of Classic FM filter through to the bathroom. Rachmaninov. *Brief Encounter* – best movie ever:

'I love you. I love you. You love me too. It's no use pretending it hasn't happened 'cause it has.'

Aah! Deep warm water. Sinking. Down, down . . .

From afar, I hear the warning snap of door latches. A metallic crash signals her entry, and foam-crested waves lap dangerously near the edge as she towers over, forcing me into the steep curve of the bath.

'What's this?' she says, thrusting her deeply grooved face towards mine.

'Hello,' I say, shaking from sudden exposure and a rush of cold air. 'What's up? Have you –– '

'What's up?' she roars. 'You mean you don't know?'

'Sorry, no,' I say, shrinking away from the bubbling face.

'Is there a cup of tea waiting? Do I get a "Hello darling, what sort of a day have you had?"? No, you're lying in the bath!'

And with a mighty scream The Witch rushes from the room.

Now it's an earlier time, and The Witch stands at my door with a suitcase and a sexy body.

'I've come to live with you,' she says, pushing past me. 'I like your house, especially the bedroom. And I'll want frequent sex in back alleys, lay-bys and quiet wooded lanes.'

'Come in,' I say, smitten by her grin. 'I want you – forever.'

I approach the kitchen from where I hear a prolonged conversation with her pet rat who flashes a "Sorry – you too?" look when I enter.

'Well – have you thought about it?' she says, not looking up from the avocado whose skin sobs from her vigorous scrubbing.

'I'm not sure what there is to — '

'I won't stand for — ' but what she won't stand for is lost in the high-pitched spin of the Hotpoint where The Witch washes single items twice daily on full cycle. Straight from body to machine – the laundry basket remains empty.

I watch an old man shuffle past, making for the Sun Room. Perhaps once my height, he is stooped and unsteady. In front of him, using both hands, he supports a worn, metal tray holding a teapot which slides to and fro in its spillings. He looks familiar, not unlike my ageing father.

'Your tea, sir. Your tea, sir,' the man mutters, as if rehearsing lines.

He returns with the remains of a breakfast, the leathery fried egg intact, blackened bacon and sausage barely touched.

A Hoover whines. The hunched Witch dashes past, thrusting the machine into edges and corners with a stabbing action, a morning and night ritual keeping the carpet like a manicured lawn.

Through the window I see the old man stagger down the garden. Straining upwards, he places duvet covers and giant towels on the washing line, careful not to disturb the single black bra. The large-handled pegs are specially designed for his bent fingers.

··· My Pink Path ···

I'd always had this fear of a wino turning up. The board by my front gate had worked so far:

> # NO WINOS

But what if they couldn't read, or it was a reformed wino entitled to walk past it conscience-free.

'Spare a few pence for a Diet Coke, Mr?'

The brick path leading to the front door turns deep pink when it's wet. And it was doing so now – on a glorious evening with the cottage glowing in spring sunshine and not a cloud to be seen. This wasn't a freak event you could tell your grandchildren about, like fish falling out of the sky. The heavy shower was flowing from the gap at the bottom of the man's trousers where they hung short of the unmatching boots planted resolutely against my doorstep.

My bike and I were late for a pint of Old Speckled Hen at the Horseshoes. I'd spent five minutes trying to persuade him to go away, but he wouldn't budge. He'd clearly taken umbrage when I refused him a room, and decided to pay me anyway – in kind. His eyes glazed over in the act – that's what flummoxed me.

'Bed,' he'd said when I opened the door, though it had come out more like an 'Ugh' through the small hole in the middle of his detritus-flecked beard. In the bits of face that weren't covered it was hard to tell where the weather-beating ended and the grime began.

'Er, no, sorry,' I said, closing the door, slowly so as not to appear impolite.

'Room,' he said. 'They said . . . ugh ugh.'

I wasn't sure if he was foreign or whether his talking ability was behind his chronological age. If he was from abroad, and his multi-layered woolly shirts and thick-knit jumpers were anything to go by, it must be considerably colder where he comes from. I reckoned the shredded waterproof over-trousers and the holes between the knitted bits would at least allow plenty of air to circulate.

'She – ugh ugh ugh.'

I start piecing things together. The landlady at The Bridge had phoned earlier.

'Have you got a room for the night?' she'd said. 'A man on business. We can't help.'

Lesley seemed an amenable sort. Martin had done a lot of work for her since she took over the pub, so I got the impression she'd be good to do business with. We'd agreed to send each other customers, just as I did with other local B&Bs once I'd visited them and could be confident about passing people on. The overflow system worked well and meant there was always a chance of filling a vacant room at the last minute.

'I'll send him straight up,' she'd said.

Nearly three hours later I'd forgotten about the man, assuming he'd made other arrangements. After all, it was only five minutes drive from the village, and twenty walking.

But I realise that the person before me with a greasy backpack and a bulging plastic bag in each hand *is* the "man on business". From the rusting fish slice, battered spirit level and other random items hanging flimsily from his backpack, and the unravelling video cassettes spilling from his bags, I presume he's in bric-a-brac. Strange that he's heading down this road, since it only leads to Utterly Undiscovered. There'll be no market for the stuff there.

The flow from inside his right leg slows to a dribble, leaving him in a pink shape that could be Zanzibar or perhaps Bermuda on my wall chart of the British Empire. His expression changes to satisfaction and relief; mine to puckered concern.

'Room!' he says, more assertively. I feel unsettled by his blank stare and the authority he commands in so few words. I'd like to think this was sharp interpersonal skills – good listening ability, an analytical mind, knowing how to pick his moment for issuing crisp and telling statements. But the cloud of alcohol hanging in the air and the fact that he's walked straight past my "No Winos" board tells me I'm wrong.

'I think there's been a mistake,' I say, tamely.

'No! The lady – ugh . . .' and he points down the road, leaving me little room for manoeuvre.

'Well no, I **haven't** got a room. I told the lady I was full tonight, so she's misled you.'

'Ugh!' he says, raising the plastic bags and leaning towards me.

'No, I don't need any bric-a-brac, thank you.'

There's an uncomfortable silence. I'm not sure if he's mad at me or just mad. I've got away without winos for years, but now I'm faced with Hagrid from Harry Potter, only worse dressed and poorly spoken. If he **had** any money this man wouldn't fit with other guests. As for the bedroom, he'd have made Kimberley look like a saint. I feel guilty rejecting him, but it's not my fault; I've been stuffed.

He's clearly not going to move. I feel isolated and helpless – the first time I've felt incapable of resolving a customer problem without direct help from someone else. Keeping my eyes on the man, I call Chris on the cordless.

'Hello mate. A gentleman here wants a room and I've told him we're full,' I say, hoping the wino thinks I'm being considerate. 'Can you help me please?'

'I'm on the way,' he says. I didn't think he'd be able to resist a spot of private policing. Chris is the right man for the case.

He arrives, in blue uniform, five minutes later – about as much time as I can keep bluffing Hagrid.

'Is there a problem?' he says, striding purposefully towards the confused man, not easy with short legs. He gets me to spell out the story.

'Evening sir,' says Chris. 'What's your name?'

'Ugh, Billy.'

'Okay Billy. There's been a misunderstanding.'

'Room, ugh, room ugh,' he says, pointing in various directions, agitatedly.

His resistance weakens as Chris tunes in to crackling voices on his walkie-talkie, pretending to seek back-up.

'Over and out,' he says. 'Sorry Billy, you'll have to go back down to the village – come on,' and he points him in the right direction. At first Billy doesn't move, but with Chris's uniformed encouragement he slowly retreats to the pavement and shuffles away, stopping to look back from time to time, less in defiance than disbelief.

'That's it, that's the way,' says Chris, nudging him along a foot at a time.

His departure is painstaking, and I can see why it took him so long to get here. Eventually he disappears round the bend.

'Thanks ever so much, Chris.'

'Pleasure, mate. Radio usually works. He's harmless enough.'

'I'll get some beers in a second,' I say, reaching for the disinfectant and keying the Bridge's number into my phone.

··· Bins, Bins ···

'Bins, bins,' witters The Witch, as she rushes past with a black plastic sack, a snake of steam in her wake.

'You did them earlier,' I say.

Seeing a small, crumpled ball of paper at the bottom of a waste basket, she removes the plastic bin liner and puts in a new one. Her yellow gloves dart about in the dimly lit room like fluorescent frogs at night.

'You *know* I don't like anything in the bins,' she says, heading off to the other rooms.

The doorbell sounds. I see a bow-legged old man unlocking a line of bolts and chains with the anticipation of opening a well-wrapped present. Against the light that rushes into the dark hallway, I watch a young couple step back, their smiles dropping away as they see the long arms hanging limp and the head lolling to one side between arched shoulders.

'Can I help you?' I hear him say, with a tired drawl. The couple scurry away as if it's the wrong house. The old man closes the door and melts into the ether.

The Witch returns to dispose of her meagre pickings in the outside dustbin. Back in the kitchen she assiduously wipes sausages with paper roll and places them on a clean plate lined with more paper roll, and covers them with another piece while the grill heats up.

'I want my money from the cottage,' says a new voice. A woman like Debbie materialises between me and The Witch. 'I said you could stay but I didn't agree to a Witch moving in.'

'Tell her she can whistle for it,' says The Witch, with a frightening chuckle.

Another woman appears, all pencil skirt and shoulder pads.

'My client wishes you to place Cricklewood Cottage on the market,' she says, waving a piece of paper at me.

'Over my dead body,' says The Witch, refusing to address anyone directly.

The two women smile at the prospect and disappear as quickly as they came, leaving The Witch exasperated and a letter in my hand.

'Well? Whose side are you on?' she yells, puffed up fit to explode.

'I'll think about it,' I say.

A burst of invective gushes from The Witch's distended mouth.

'You're not to talk to her! Do you hear me?'

'But she's my daughter's mother, so I need —— '

'I don't care! You'll have nothing to do with her!'

'But I can't —— '

'And you can stop seeing your daughter too! She'll be out of your life soon enough – make it now!'

'But she's seven, for heaven's sake!'

The Witch waves a dagger-shaped kitchen knife in the air.

'You'd be surprised what could happen to this cottage if I put my mind to it,' she says, with a practised smirk.

Outside I see a frail figure leaning flat on a ladder, wiping silt-caked, Georgian-style windows with a filthy cloth. Between each pane he pauses to catch his breath. Below, the car park is colonised with earth and matted weeds, and off this leads a jagged concrete path, shaded by rampant sycamores and ashes and thick with emerald moss.

The old man comes down the ladder with painstaking attention to each rung, and steps gingerly along the path to the garden at the back. There he surveys a row of arches, slumped at different angles, at the base of each arch the cracked, blackened stumps of old roses suffocated by nettles and goose grass.

At the end of the row I see him enter a clearing, where a bright yellow bulldozer is flattening an old building made of cardboard and matchsticks, and space-suited workmen are throwing slabs of white material into a pink skip. A giant glass frame stands erect for a while, before toppling over and shattering into millions of pieces.

'Wake up, mate. We're he-urr.'

'Hm?'

'Yorr home.'

'Oh, right – thanks,' I say, getting my bearings.

'Take care – and thanks for the curry.'

'That's okay. I enjoyed it. Thanks for a good evening.'

I was back in one piece – but at one point I'd begun to wonder. Chris had jumped a chicane on the wrong side of a traffic island in Town Walls. I'd had one of those "Did that really just happen?" moments, but didn't like to say anything. Perhaps I should have guessed by the speed he approached it. It's a blessing there was no-one about, but I'd wondered what was in store for the rest of the journey.

It had suited me to let him drive, even though I normally avoided mixing cars and alcohol. My metabolism had been slowed by four pints of Felinfoel in the Hop and Friar and a King Prawn Bhuna at the Parveen. After the chicane I closed my eyes and hoped for the best. There was thick fog in Plox Green; Chris said he'd hit it just outside Shroosbury, and I'd like to think it made him slow down.

He'd phoned earlier that Sunday to suggest a curry, and I'd agreed on the condition that I buy the meal as a thank you for helping me out with Billy the wino a few weeks earlier. He'd sounded distracted, and later the cause became clear. Though he wouldn't go into detail, there'd been a suggestion he should take early retirement at work, which Chris wasn't happy about. But it was the news that he was splitting up with his wife after more than twenty-five years that took me by surprise. I barely knew Julie, but they'd seemed happy enough on the few occasions I saw them together. I remembered her raised eyebrows when Chris, as he often did, talked about his celebrity contacts. Apparently, Cliff Richard had invited them to his barbecue in the Algarve one year, and Chris regularly chummed up with Pete Postlethwaite and shared recipes with Nick Nairn on trips to Glasgow. No doubt there were other stars I hadn't heard about from his fifty something years, bearing in mind I'd only known him for nine of them.

Their break-up was none of my business. I assumed that, like me and Debbie, the marriage had simply run its course. That evening I offered what support I could, though I'm not sure his Formula 1 tactics in town were the best way of saying thanks.

Things moved very quickly after that. Later in the summer Chris wrote off his high spec Honda on the M69 near Leicester. There were no injuries, but I imagine the trauma was a major turning point – the sleek, silver classic had been his pride and joy. Shortly afterwards he was released from the force, already planning to live in Cyprus where, apparently, he had contacts who'd find him work for the BBC. By the end of the year he was gone.

Chris was one of several friends to leave in 2002. Richard, who'd done so much work on the cottage, moved to Bournemouth with his family, leaving Martin, a skilled carpenter and jack of most trades, to carry on with any work that needed doing at the B&B, as well as odd jobs for Debbie at Lily Cottage.

Another Chris I'd befriended, with a son called Jack whom Lily had played with as a toddler, also left with his family for a new life in Surrey. Bill the Vicar was about to take up a new role elsewhere, and the time had come for Jim and Barbara at the Horseshoes to hang up their beer mats and retire to Shroosbury.

It was also the year Violet died. At last re-united with Jack after twelve lonely years, she lies in Minsterley Cemetery, in a tidy grave with a black marble headstone engraved "John William Jones 1990 and Violet Hannah Jones 2002". With no children of their own, they'd been buried alongside Hannah Roberts 1954, a niece who'd died young. Gladys was in a separate family grave.

Sadly, I'd been able to offer little support to Violet in the few years since Gladys had passed away in the Care Home. Before then, John or I had driven her to the Home for afternoon visiting, for which she'd insisted on slipping us a fiver. But without Gladys, Violet changed from being a desolate figure to a virtual recluse. It was as if she'd been so conditioned by their three-way existence – her, Jack and Gladys – that her reason for living had gone.

Kneeling or lying on the living room floor in her camel overcoat in front of a two-bar fire was her daily and often nightly routine. If I saw her at the giant screen, it was as if she couldn't see me. Jack's brother called with basic supplies, and a nephew and niece visited, but she refused to accept any help either personally or with the building that was falling apart around her.

On the rare occasions she answered the door to me, she left the chain on and briefly peered through the gap before closing it while I was still talking. Meg was sometimes allowed in, but couldn't do much. She said there was damp and mould everywhere, some of which I could see through the giant screen – peeling wallpaper, blackened ceiling and fungus growing from the floor. Towards the end, weeds and small ferns were starting to grow from gaps under the skirting boards. Violet never allowed anyone to deal with this and was eventually found lying dead by the fire. It's like she'd been waiting to die in the house her Jack built.

Though my social life was now built around the pub and people I'd met through Network, the friends who left the area had all been important in my life, and I missed them when they'd gone. Whilst I wasn't yet ready to follow suit, their departures so close together did start me thinking about my own future. After all, nothing is forever.

··· Hounded ···

'Are you going?' a farmer in a crinkled, tweed jacket asks me in the Horseshoes.

'Going where?' I say.

'On the march,' he says, in a pinched voice.

'What march?'

He's not impressed. I get the feeling that everyone living in the countryside is expected to buy in to the ideals of the Countryside Alliance, and that failure to do so is betraying the cause.

The Liberty and Livelihood March in London had been postponed because of the 2001 foot-and-mouth outbreak, but on 22nd September a year later, thousands of people are due to descend on the capital by car, or in one of the estimated two thousand five hundred coaches and thirty charter trains.

Ostensibly the march is to draw attention to the many threats to rural life. But the headline grabber is fox-hunting with dogs. That's the, ahem, sport where a dozen or so red-coated, pompous people on tall, expensive horses, and a large pack of hyped-up hounds charge across someone else's land intent on ripping a small, red-coated animal to shreds.

I could understand catching foxes if it was done humanely and was in the natural order of things, say to eat them in order to survive. For that reason, shooting game has its place; for so long as I choose to eat pheasant or venison I can't really grumble. Even then, there's something about the shooters and their guns that leaves me uncomfortable. On the one hand I feel distanced by wealthy people pursuing their interests so single-mindedly, on the other by those seeking pickings more furtively. In a rare foray to the Crown and Anchor, I overhear three shifty-looking men at the far end of the bar making plans that sound less than kosher.

'Dunna take no notice of him. He won't say nothing,' one of them said.

'Plenty of pheasants in there,' said another. 'No-one'd know.'

It was the way they discussed their intentions so brazenly that intimidated me. I wouldn't have wanted to come across them in the dark – with double-barrelled shotguns. It was the same exclusion I'd felt overhearing the three ruddy-faced farmers bragging in the Horseshoes during foot-and-mouth – except they were posh and the pheasant trio weren't.

In Minsterley the attitude towards the march is low key, but near Bishops Castle, where there's a Hunt kennels, roadside posters condemning the proposed ban are much in evidence. Many people gain a living from the Hunt, and ten coaches alone will be travelling from this normally quiet Shropshire town. Waiting for Lily outside the school gate I soak up local opinion like a sponge, and hold my own counsel.

On the big day, from the comfort of my sofa, nursing a giant mug of tea, I can see on television just how big the operation is, and why it could only take place on a Sunday. An endless sea of chanting faces fills every street, hunting horns blaring, whistles shrieking, bagpipes droning. A scratch orchestra with backing choir – better than any sedative.

The Witch pours a large white wine and takes a slug before slamming the glass on the coffee table.

'Right, who is she?' she says through bared teeth.

'Who is who?' I say, resting on the sofa to unlace my shoes.

'You *know* who I mean!'

'I really don't ––'

'How dare you treat me like that!'

'Like what?' I say, calmly.

'You talked to the woman opposite all evening and completely ignored me,' she says, her face boiling into bubbly blotches. 'So come on – who is she?'

Her measured tone feels more menacing than when she shouts.

'I don't know her any more than you,' I say. 'We only just met; one of Barry's friends, I assume. And I *was* trying to include you.'

'You're lying. There's something going on – I know it,' says The Witch. 'And I'm going to find out!' She sinks the wine and storms out.

The scene is more tiresome than threatening. In the kitchen I make tea to cut through the Chinese dinner still lying heavy. The Witch's attack defies logic, but there is nothing I can say.

Through to the Sun Room I can see a shrunken old man in a matted dressing gown and threadbare slippers, muttering as he lays places for breakfast. A fork clatters to the floor and in a series of rehearsed moves he lowers himself to retrieve it. The towelling gown is handy for polishing the juice tumblers, opaque after years in the dishwasher. The house lights flicker as he fiddles with the dimmer, then he disappears in the darkness.

The Witch appears in a negligee that finishes in the middle where her legs start.

'I'm ready now. You can come and make it up to me,' she says, unashamedly sharing her dark shapes and feminine contours.

I have nothing to make up, but there is little I can do.

Tea's gone cold again – I never do drink it in time. I hear Rob McElwee saying the marchers have been lucky with the weather, but have to wait till the evening news to find out there were an estimated four hundred thousand marchers. I like to think a lot were supporting rural issues like public transport and Post Offices, and that it wasn't just wealthy people trying to protect a cruel sport.

A banner says: 'Blair – ban hunting and we'll boot you out'.

I'm sure Tony will make a pretty good job of that himself – eventually.

⋯ George and Tony ⋯

George	How ya doing, my little playmate?
Tony	Not bad, sir. Do you think we did okay?
George	Your boys were just great, Tony – did us proud!
Tony	Hit 'em where it hurts, eh? Gimme five!
George	Yup! They wanna come back for more – we'll be ready.

That's two Gulf Wars I've fitted into my time at Cricklewood Cottage. Six months on, the questions are being asked. I like good satire, and from my deep, leather armchair in the back room of The Wheatsheaf, the Shroosbury Players are making a great job of Iraq. All the better seen through heavy eyes and a haze of Carlsberg lager.

Tony	Me too, sir. (*Pause*) Are you absolutely certain it was legal though, going in like that?
George	Working for democracy, Tony. Had to be done.
Tony	Yes I know – but was it legal?
George	You questioning my judgement, Tony? You saying I was wrong?
Tony	No, no – you know best.
George	Don't you forget that, boy.
Tony	But did we actually find any weapons of mass destruction?
George	Not the point, Tony, not the point.
Tony	If you say so, sir. I'm a bit worried they won't believe me though.
George	Had no time for the goddam warmonger, Tony. Gave him a last chance: 'Don't want you no more – now get outta here!' I said. Can't get much clearer than that, boy.

'I don't love you and don't want you here,' I tell The Witch. 'Please go.'

'I'll go when I'm good and ready,' she says. 'I know you love me really.'

'No I don't.'

'You don't get rid of me that easily.'

'I want you to leave. I don't want to be with you and I don't want you living here.'

'Why not?' asks The Witch, sharply.

'Because I have no feelings for you.'

'Then why did you want to stop in a lay-by on Saturday night? That looked like feelings to me.'

'I didn't. You made me.'

'How could I *make* you?'

'Because you threatened a scene at the cottage if I didn't.'

'Don't tell me you didn't enjoy it. I could tell you loved me.'

'It's not what I wanted.'

'You're cruel. You hated Benson and now you hate me!'

'I didn't hate Benson. He died naturally, like other rats. And I don't *hate* you.'

'You still love me – don't you?'

'No.'

'It's *her*, isn't it?'

'Who?'

'Her – that woman!'

'It's nobody. I don't feel comfortable with *you* around me.'

'Nobody will buy the place, you know. I'll make sure of that.'

'You won't.'

'You realise how easy it would be. I'm staying. We'll both move to the sea.'

'We won't. Can you make other plans, please. It's six months since I asked you.'

The Witch stomps to the fridge and returns with a tub of yoghurt, which she picks at quickly, whimpering between spoonfuls.

I see a soaking wet, old man, weighed down with Tesco bags coming through the back door. At the sound of dripping water he looks up to the brown ceiling stains where the kitchen has pulled away from the cottage, giving free passage to rain and a new door for the soaring mouse population.

I follow him past The Witch, who digs angrily into her empty yoghurt, scraping along surfaces already cleaner than a cat would leave them. Pausing and panting on his way up the stairs, the old man sets new tablets of soap in the Bow Room, making a note to tackle the mould round the bath and get the cracked toilet bowl replaced.

'I'll see myself out!' screams The Witch, rushing past me with two suitcases as I come back down. 'Don't think this is the end!'

The front door wobbles on its hinges before slamming shut in her draught. As she drives off, a man like Martin arrives to change the locks.

··· The Good, the Bad and the Ugly ···

If I'd kept a diary, the entry for Sunday 30th May 2004 would have looked like this:

Six minutes to go, Iwelumo is brought down in the area. Leon Knight steps up to the penalty spot for his twenty-seventh strike of the season. Goal! Bristol City 0 – Brighton and Hove Albion 1, and promotion to the newly christened Championship. Could life get any better? A day out with forty thousand committed Brighton fans at the magnificent Cardiff Millennium Stadium, and a perfect outcome.

After post-match drinks my pals pile into their minibus, Sussex-bound. I'd love to be with them. Instead, as I shuffle forward outside Cardiff Station a testosterone-drenched Bristol City fan, half my height and twice my width, wearing a ridiculous, red pork-pie hat with "Loser" across the front, thinks I'm busting the queue.

'Oh no you don't!' he says, Bristol fashion but not quite ship-shape. He picks me up like I was a feather pillow and moves me back up the row. The hat should have read: "Poor Loser". I decide he's probably from a poor part of Bristol too (if there's a rich one), but I don't stop to check. Luckily my train is on a different platform.

I see a few pockets of ex-pat Albion fans on the Shroosbury train, sharing my elation. The day's excesses and the warmth of a crowded carriage soon catch up on me.

'So – now a football match is more important than me, is it?'

'I thought you'd gone.'

'I said you wouldn't get rid of me that easily.'

'What do you want?'

'What about the weekend in Teignmouth you promised?'

'I really don't see the point ——'

'You promised!' screams The Witch, a scarlet boil splitting open on the hook of her nose. Other passengers look over as she mops at the grey rivulet and wrings her hands like she's trying to wash out their skin colour.

'It's too late.'

'All right, take me for a drink then.'

'Why?'

'Because I know you still want me.'

'I don't want you.'

The Witch flicks vigorously at the underside of her handbag where it has rested on the floor.

'Show me you want me.'

'I don't want you.'

'I'm going to the toilet – follow me!' she says, more an instruction than a request.

'I don't need the toilet. And I don't want you.'

'How dare you!' she screeches. 'After all I gave you.'

'Took.'

All self control abandoned, The Witch grabs at my arms in a sort of wrestling hold, tugging them back and forth while emitting little frothing sounds from the back of her skinny throat.

'Steady on!' says a man sitting next to me. 'Are you all right?'

'I'm fine,' I say, nonchalantly wiping away the dribble tracking down my blue and white shirt. 'Sorry, did I disturb you?'

My carriage has thinned to the man and me. The Train Manager announces Hereford.

'Not really. Bad dream, was it*?*'

'You *could* say that.'

'Spot of bother?'

'It's all right. She's gone now.'

··· My Basil Meets Mr Grey ···

'Dad, there's a parrot in the Rose Room.'

Lily, nearly eight and three quarters, had gone to top up the room trays with teabags and Millac Maid cartons, her latest school holiday job. She rushes back to the kitchen with the news.

'All right, Lil,' I say, thinking it's a trick. She knows from the sign at the gate, next to my "No Winos" board, that parrots are banned:

NO NOISY PARROTS

'No, there really is, dad! Come and look!'

I follow her up, imagining she's seen a lapwing on the roof of the Sun Room, which runs off below. There'd been a flock of them on the field the last few days; perhaps one of them had even flown in through an open window.

The carpet is coated with paper pellets, like a badly run classroom. A scuffle behind the door leads me to the parrot.

'I don't believe it!'

'Hello Mr Grey,' I say.

'How do you know it's a man parrot, dad?'

'He looks like one, don't you think?'

'I suppose so. He's very quiet for a parrot.'

He stares, head cocked, challenging me to look away first. He wins easily.

'So – you're on the run, eh Mr Grey? Drug dealing, false-bottomed cage, holing up till things go quiet? Pellet wraps – street value five grand? Good cover!'

'Why is he here, dad? You don't allow parrots, do you?'

'Perhaps the parrot kennels were full, darling. They might have gagged him and smuggled him upstairs when I wasn't looking.'

A nod like a Churchill dog on a car parcel shelf tells me I'm right. He looks me up and down before executing three revolutions and a full pike, double twist dismount. His floor is furnished with sunflower seeds and shredded paper, perfect play material for the tedium of a one-roomed cage.

'I suppose your minders said, "Don't worry about the mess; My Basil will clear it up", eh?'

He stops nodding, and a different kind of pellet drops to the floor behind him.

'I'll take that as a "yes", shall I? What am I – your skivvy? You do realise I could truss you up and have you for dinner?'

'Dad, the people in this room said funny things when I took the toast.'

'What sort of things?'

'Well, they copied each other. When she said "Hello Lily", he said it too. And when he said "Ooh, toast", she said it back.'

'You mean like "Ooh toast, ooh toast"?'

'Yes. I think they're a bit funny.'

'Hm, maybe you've got something, Lil. Come to think of it, when I was waiting to take their order, they both went "Caw, caw". I thought they were admiring the menu.'

'What do you think's wrong with them?'

'I think they might have got like their pet. They say dog owners get like their dogs, and I think it might be the same with parrots. They've learnt to speak his language – parrot-speak.'

'But Mr Grey doesn't say much anyway. Do humans really do parrot-speak, dad?'

'It looks like it, Lil. Perhaps we should join in. At breakfast tomorrow we could each say "Good morning" to them twice. It'd sound like that Beatles song we keep playing – "Good Morning, Good Morning".'

I hear a chuckle, but it's not Lily, it's Mr Grey as he picks at the paper scraps beneath him.

'Ouch! Did you just spit that? Watch it – I'm a Black Belt, First Dan, you know!'

'Dad, this paper's got writing on it,' says Lily, unravelling one of the pellets.

'Where, let's have a look? "Yoghurt – fruit – and –– " Hey! My breakfast menu!'

'Outrageous! Projectile hawking my menu! I'll show you hawking, Mr Grey! There are plenty outside who'd love a tasty parrot!'

'Shall we see if he wants to come out, Lily?'

'Is that all right? What if he gets away?'

'That's okay. They've sneaked him in when they shouldn't, so if he disappears, they can't really own up to having him.'

'But what about the cage?'

'Oh, we'll get rid of that and clear up this mess. It'll be like he was never here in the first place.'

'Parrot? What parrot? You never mentioned a parrot. Not even the one you sneaked past the "No Noisy Parrots" sign after blatantly distracting me asking for tea and garibaldis.'

'Let's try, shall we? Fresh air will do him good. Out you come, Mr Grey. Good boy. Careful – wait till the window's open. No – stop bashing yourself! Wait, Mr Grey!'

'Dad, I can hear those people downstairs,' says Lily through a cloud of feathers. 'They must have come back for him.'

'Come here, you little devil! Get back in that cage!'

'My Basil, My Basil,' he cries.

'Dad, the parrot's talking now.'

'I know! Quick, try and catch him!'

'My Basil, My Basil,' he says, louder.'

'They're coming up the stairs, dad!'

'MY BASIL, MY BASIL.'

'Shhhh!'

··· Four Latvians ···

The uncertainty next door was worrying. After Violet died, her dilapidated bungalow was put up for sale, a prime target for demolition and development. Whenever I heard the roar of a powerful vehicle, I expected it to be as much a yellow bulldozer as one of Wake's sludge tankers. But the lay of the land and its proximity to the brook made it hard to develop, and ownership quickly passed through several small builders.

Two years on, and the latest owner, seeing there was no profit in the site, rented the bungalow to four immigrant workers from Latvia who'd taken temporary employment at Minsterley Creamery. When their jobs ended they found work at the Muller factory in Market Drayton, where they were taken daily by minibus. The demand for milk-based products was relentless, though Minsterley Creamery itself was threatened with closure in the face of tough competition from Muller and the Dairy Crest factory at Crudgington, the other side of Shroosbury.

During our occasional contact in broken English, the two young Latvian couples seemed happy and friendly, and in the remaining summer months made the bungalow their home as best they could. But it had been empty for two years and untouched for fourteen, and as winter approached John excused himself to call in. He found them living in atrocious conditions. With only two small electric bar fires to service the bungalow, there was nothing to stave off the damp, and John said the air smelt thick with fungal growth. The peeling wallpaper from Violet's days, which had been fixed back loosely by the landlord, was rolling off, and fresh mould had settled over the cursory attempts to scrape off earlier blackness, leaving a tie-dye effect across the Artex ceilings.

The rent of more than a hundred pounds each a month was excessive considering the condition of the place. John offered to contact Environmental Health, but the Latvians were reluctant for him to do so; instead he lent them additional convector heaters to alleviate the wetness and make it marginally more comfortable.

And like the rest of us, they were blissfully ignorant about the drainage. None of the builders who'd owned the plot could find where the sewage went. Severn Trent Water confirmed the property wasn't connected to mains sewage, there was no sign of a septic tank and I'd never seen a waste collection vehicle calling. I began to see what Jack meant when he said, 'That's the way round here. Everyone up the valley does it.'

The Latvians were uncomplaining. Either they felt vulnerable to eviction or were used to similar conditions back home. They didn't even have the benefit of a view across our garden to the Stiperstones – which I'd like to think had lifted Violet's spirits from time to time – because a decent period after the bungalow became empty, Martin had erected a six foot fence for me at the border of the two properties.

··· Dream Over ···

At 12.49 on 6th July 2005 I danced a jig in the long border at Boscobel House. But my hop through the hollyhocks was nothing compared to the leaping up and down of Sebastian Coe and his team in Singapore after the following statement by Jacques Rogge:

'The International Olympic Committee has the honour of announcing that the games of the 30th Olympiad in 2012 are awarded to – the City of London.'

Not that I paid much attention to the Olympics. Perhaps I'd tune in to watch celebrity athletes or Brits with a good chance, but otherwise I found the two or three week's TV relentless. I allowed myself the jig because this was a rare moment; let's face it, Britain winning *any* major event is to be celebrated.

And the feel-good factor perfectly matched my personal plans. I was about to go on my first summer foreign holiday for over seventeen years. The sense of freedom doing such a commonplace thing was overwhelming, all the more so for knowing I'd soon be leaving Cricklewood Cottage.

For the last couple of years, with the cottage on the market, I'd kept the B&B ticking over and enjoyed hosting my regular guests. Poignantly, some of the last were Tony and Anne from London. This wonderful couple had been a mainstay from the start, revelling in the cottage and garden the way we'd intended. On their last night, over a celebratory dinner at the Lion Hotel in Shroosbury, we reminisced about the past and pondered the future. They'd always taken an interest in my personal and business wellbeing, and I would look forward to visiting them in their Enfield home.

The hydrofoil was entering Venice on a day trip from Croatia when my mobile signal returned, flashing an exciting text:

'Contracts exchanged – completion end of July.'

My day exploring the waterfronts and hidden canals of this wonderful "floating city" was rife with anticipation, not only for what I saw but for what lay ahead at home.

In *The Innkeeper's Diary*, John Fothergill listed his requirements for 'keeping a good Inn'. He was spot on. I too had worked fourteen to sixteen hours a day – but with freedom to decide, and lots of time off in the winter. We too had had a mind for the tiniest detail – a great breakfast menu and Debbie's touches around the house. And we too had planned the venture carefully, extended wisely, and taken the risk of shedding people and pets along the way. My Basil had even enjoyed a natural love for the job, one up on Basil Fawlty who consistently fell at this hurdle.

But seventeen years is a long time, and I was glad to be leaving the B&B. Undoubtedly I'd miss working for myself and the sense of achievement from seeing guests enjoy the cottage so much. I'd fulfilled my ambition a hundred times over, and whilst I still enjoyed having people to stay, it had become harder after I increased to three days a week with English Heritage, taking on the gardens at Much Wenlock Priory and Boscobel House. And of course the cottage was only half mine; seven years was time enough for Debbie to wait for her share.

It was the garden that tilted the balance. Looking after English Heritage gardens was a great job, but it made tending my own something of a busman's holiday. The workload reached a peak in all of them during spring and summer, which was also the time I had most guests. I'd get home from a physically hard day at one of the gardens and spot things in my own that needed attention. My pride in keeping them all looking good made this tortuous. Whilst I would never have let any go to seed, I was starting to feel the aches and pains of Anno Domini, my overworked limbs themselves starting to go over.

Technology too was passing me by. The growing demand for online reservations, plastic cards and websites was not my world. If I'd stayed, I'd have had to invest a lot of money to survive. And I'd have been exposed to the growing phenomenon of internet review sites like *Trip Advisor*. I was already using these to book holidays for myself, but I always wondered who wrote the reviews and whether competitors might be tempted to place negative information about B&Bs they'd never seen. I'm not sure I could have handled that.

I did buy into a stock website (*Smoothhound*) for the last few years, successfully using my colour brochure to attract people online. And I tiptoed into internet connection with Bush TV, a set-top box that gave access via my television monitor. It was ponderous and unreliable technology but at least I could declare an email address and appear businesslike, and in *my* little world it made me feel right up there with the technophiles. It's a blessing that most of my customers were Luddites, preferring the old-fashioned way – letters and payment by cash or cheque. So I got away with it – just! And after the incident with the Woodwards, who'd had to stay at Colleen's, I bought a Brother word processor for guest correspondence, which looked more professional and made bookings clearer.

I also embraced mobile phones. My greatest concern had been a loss of trade through missed calls. But a mobile phone and subscription to BT's Call Diversion service meant that, at the click of a button, calls to Cricklewood Cottage could be diverted to the mobile. No doubt managing my diary in public irritated friends and fellow travellers.

'Dad, why did you just rush into that alleyway?'

'To get away from the background noise, Lily.'

'You looked weird crouching down writing.'

'Thanks Lily.'

But the system was a godsend, *and* I managed it without having a bullfrog as an incoming call tone or ever saying out loud: 'I'm on the train.'

Fifty-one prospective buyers had viewed the cottage, and the couple who bought it were the very first. It was just what they were looking for, but they hadn't yet sold their house in Southampton, which meant that over the next two years we had to suffer fifty rejections:

'I hadn't realised it was so close to the road.' (20)

'We've got small children; the brook's a worry.' (7)

'There's a lot of garden, isn't there?' (5)

Concrete it over then, madam.

'It's the sloping ceilings; my husband's tall.' (3)

'Our Georgian daining-table will be a bit tate in the Sun Room.' (1)

No further contact. (14)

Rude.

I can still keep a good statistic.

When the agent phoned out of the blue to give the go-ahead from the Southampton couple, I had one of those "Yes!" moments. The final throes were swift. Such was their commitment, the buyers' response to the surveyor's report suggesting the cottage would fall down by the weekend, was:

'That's rubbish! You know what surveyors are like.'

There's always an ideal buyer.

Seventeen years exactly since I opened Cricklewood Cottage to the discerning public, and today everything that's gone in comes out – in eight hours and three white van loads.

My brilliant neighbours, Geoff and Colleen, call in to say goodbye. Colleen hugs me like a long-lost friend and gives me a bottle of sparkling elderflower wine and three specimen geraniums for my new home. John and Meg come over with a large box of mixed vegetables; when either of us had been away over recent years, we'd minded each other's gardens, as good friends should. They'd soon be getting to know their new neighbours, as well as keeping an eye on the Latvians. I'll miss all these lovely people, but I know I'll see them again when I'm back visiting Lily.

Debbie calls to collect boxes of well-thumbed gardening books from the Reading Room shelves. She takes a tray of rare plant cuttings and her favourite pieces of art deco.

'Do you remember the white plates?' she asks.

'Ah yes, the white plates and saucers,' I say, re-living our Brighton days. 'Still got them under plant pots.'

Once we'd decided on running a B&B, we'd started collecting white, second-hand crockery from junk shops, believing that as long as it was tasteful, guests would approve. Even though it never reached the table, rounding up random crockery in Brighton was a simple way of getting in the mood for business. That none of it matched didn't occur to us at the time.

'We'll still see the daffodils,' she says, plaintively.

In our first autumn, we'd spent two days on hands and knees planting two thousand bulbs in the grass verge outside. Every spring they were like a beacon as you came round the corner towards the cottage.

After a final look at the garden Debbie disappears down the pink path, visibly upset. Seven years have passed, yet her time at the cottage remains deeply ingrained; for Debbie too it is the end of an era. Yet it's also the start of another – she's to marry Martin, which means Lily will have a great stepdad.

'Are you sure you'll be all right?' says my dad on the phone.

'If I'm not after fifty-seven years, I never will be.' I say. 'I'm just Drifting down to Herefordshire to see how things go.'

Mum and dad had stopped visiting in the last year, finding it too far to drive and more difficult to get around. I suspect they also felt uncomfortable with people viewing the cottage, and wanted to preserve memories of how it was in the early days.

'Remember – I'm here if there's anything you want.'

'I know you are. Thanks, Dad.'

I remove the Bed & Breakfast sign, which won't be needed; perhaps it'll make a good plant stand. And I take my last load in the battered, high roof Transit to my temporary digs in Bishops Castle, and beyond that Ledbury, far enough to make a new life yet close enough to Lily.

Beside me on the passenger seat are two chunky Visitors Books, a lasting record of those who shared our home; and tucked inside, the thank you letters and magazine articles that spoke so generously of what we did.

'Aar, ee'm going the wrong way,' a worried farmer says out loud, watching the B&B bloke turn left off the pink-gravelled car park and edge past the wailing crowds towards the country crossroads. 'There'm only Utterly Undiscovered up there.'

fineleaf